I have been driven many times to my knees by the overwhelming conviction that I had nowhere else to go.

TIMELESS GRACE

Prayers for Every Occasion

— ◦ ❈ ◦ —

ELLEN BANKS ELWELL

Tyndale House Publishers, Inc.
Carol Stream, Illinois

Visit Tyndale online at www.tyndale.com.

TYNDALE and Tyndale's quill logo are registered trademarks of Tyndale House Publishers, Inc. *Living Expressions* and the Living Expressions logo are trademarks of Tyndale House Publishers, Inc.

Prayers for Every Occasion

Designed by Jennifer Phelps

Unless otherwise indicated, all Scripture quotations are taken from the *Holy Bible*, New Living Translation, copyright © 1996, 2004, 2015 by Tyndale House Foundation. Used by permission of Tyndale House Publishers, Inc., Carol Stream, Illinois 60188. All rights reserved.

Scripture quotations marked MSG are taken from *THE MESSAGE*, copyright © 1993, 1994, 1995, 1996, 2000, 2001, 2002 by Eugene H. Peterson. Used by permission of NavPress. All rights reserved. Represented by Tyndale House Publishers, Inc.

Scripture quotations marked NIV are taken from the Holy Bible, *New International Version*,® *NIV*.® Copyright © 1973, 1978, 1984, 2011 by Biblica, Inc.® Used by permission. All rights reserved worldwide.

Scripture quotations marked KJV are taken from the *Holy Bible*, King James Version.

For information about special discounts for bulk purchases, please contact Tyndale House Publishers at csresponse@tyndale.com, or call 1-800-323-9400.

ISBN 978-1-4964-2655-0

Printed in China

24   23   22   21   20   19   18
7   6   5   4   3   2   1

TO JIM

In you, I see God's truth and grace.

With you, I witness God's answers to prayer.

Our collaboration—in life and on this

book—is a blessing from God.

Contents

— ✦ ✦ —

During a chapel service I attended in my freshman year of college, I heard about an upcoming Urbana Student Missions Conference. John Stott was the featured speaker, and more than twelve thousand students, pastors, and missionaries were expected to attend. Desiring to go, yet not wanting to burden my parents for the cost of the event, I prayed, "God, I would really like to attend Urbana. Would you please provide the money?" I didn't mention my prayer to anyone else. As a student with no income at the time, I reasoned that if God wanted me to be at the conference, his provision would make that clear.

Several weeks later, my mom called me. "Ellen, the company you worked for over the summer just called to say that you haven't cashed your final paycheck yet."

I was puzzled. "Really? Oh, Mom, I'm *sure* I cashed or deposited all of my paychecks. But just in case, could you check my bedroom closet? I stored my paycheck stubs in a shoebox on the shelf."

I waited while my mom ran upstairs to look. A minute or so later, she was back on the phone. "Guess what I found in that shoebox!" she exclaimed. "One uncashed paycheck on top of all the stubs!"

I was amazed. I'd heard of this kind of surprise happening to other people, but not to *me*. And then I remembered . . . I had prayed that God would provide funds for me to attend Urbana, having no clue that the money could appear in the form of an uncashed check. After looking at the registration form for the conference, I realized that the amount of the uncashed paycheck my mom reported to me would not only pay for me to attend the event, it would also cover my transportation there and back.

I was gratefully humbled by God's generous provision. He had heard—and answered—my prayer with such a clear answer. With newfound confidence I signed up, even though I didn't know anyone else who was attending. Not surprisingly, I loved every minute of it.

That experience changed me significantly. Knowing that God heard my prayer bolstered my faith and prompted me to keep praying, for myself and for others. Years later, I'm more convinced than ever that God hears our petitions and provides what we need. After reading through the Bible many times, I'm also convinced that

God is the *only* one who has overcome the world and has the power to transform us from the inside out. For me, this change began by poring over the words in the Bible and pouring my heart out to God.

The best part of my day is the time I spend reading my *One Year Bible* each morning. God's Word renews my life and shapes my prayers. After reading that God created the world, I'm more mindful to thank him for things like pink hydrangeas, blue herons, or yellow corn on the cob. When I hit a snag and begin to worry, I'm reminded that since God feeds the birds who don't plant, harvest, or store food, he will certainly care for me. Pondering this promise prompts me to say, "God, please help me in this quagmire I'm facing, especially in moments when my faith is weak."

As you look through these selections, you might find phrases that describe things you've been thinking or praying about. Sometimes, listening in on another person's thoughts and words helps us make sense of our own. We're glad to know we're not alone in our journeys. Please feel free to read a prayer aloud at a gathering, use portions of prayers in a greeting card or e-mail, or adapt the wording of a prayer to better reflect your particular situation.

Arranged alphabetically by specific occasions or topics, this book contains a total of 176 prayers. All of the specific-occasion prayers are original. Others are prayers from the Bible, stanzas from hymns that can be used as prayers or even sung, and prayers said throughout history. Hopefully, you'll find some that are meaningful to your life and situation.

Over the years, I've reflected on how much my life was influenced by attending the Urbana Student Missions Conference in college. It surely sparked my interest in reading God's Word and in seeing his work being accomplished around the world. I had no idea then that as life unfolded, I would end up working alongside my husband in Christian publishing, traveling with him throughout the world, and glimpsing how God's Word changes people's lives—ours included. My prayer for you is that God's answer to one of your prayers might change your life today and impact other lives in the future.

Some people think
God does not like to
be troubled with
our constant coming
and asking. The way
to trouble God is
not to come at all.

D. L. MOODY

PART ONE

Prayers for Specific Occasions

ANNIVERSARY

———— • ————

GIVER OF LIFE AND LOVE, on my wedding anniversary,
I have much to thank you for. You have blessed me with
a husband who is thoughtful, responsible, and dependable.
In your kind providence, you've allowed us to establish a
home, grow in harmony, and serve side by side—wherever
we are.

We've collected thousands of shared memories over
the years. You've seen the times we've laughed together,
cried together, and had deep discussions about things we
have read, heard, and experienced. Through joys and sorrows, summers and winters, we've known that your presence has been with us. At times when the going has been
uncertain, we're thankful you've been alongside us, guard-
ing, guiding, and protecting. Thank you not only for our
immediate family, but also for the extended church family
and circle of friends you've blessed us with—to celebrate
with us in happy times and offer support to us in difficult
times. These people have consistently prayed for us, and
we have seen you provide all that we need.

Thank you for the unfailing love you have shown
to us, Father. May our love for you and for each other
continue to increase and be a lasting tribute to your
faithfulness.

BAPTISM OF AN ADULT

——— • ———

LORD, today I will witness the baptism of my friend and joyfully celebrate her faith. Even though I have seen many baptisms, each one I attend stirs something deep inside me. I feel joy and wonder, mixed with mystery. It's been beautiful to watch my friend's faith grow and hear her declare that she wants to follow you.

None of us can follow you perfectly, Lord Jesus. This was the case in your disciples' lives, men who sometimes failed despite their best intentions. You are the only person who never wandered, but lived in perfect fellowship with your heavenly Father. Even so, you have instructed us to embrace the act of baptism as a sign of our spiritual union with you.

On this day, Lord, make yourself known intimately to my friend, as she keeps her focus on you. Please imprint on her mind your lasting calling, and may you strengthen, guide, and continue the good work which you have begun in her life. May all of us who witness this event provide our friendship and support in the days to come. Amen.

BEDTIME

—— • ——

DEAR FATHER, "Now I lay me down to sleep, I pray the Lord my soul to keep." These words, plucked from a familiar children's prayer, still resonate with me. Somewhere deep inside me, they tap into adult-sized fears that sometimes surface in the night. Though my slumber might be disturbed by bumps and creaks, it's more often my uncertainties of the future or fears of complicated tasks and relationships that leave me tossing and turning. Yet all the while, Lord, you quietly and sovereignly watch over me. No problem or situation is unknown to you or too big for you to solve. No care or fear I have is beyond the scope of your understanding. Tonight instead of counting my worries or even counting sheep, may I rest in the countless ways you provide for me. For you are the Good Shepherd, I am your lamb, and you have promised to be with me.

> How precious are your thoughts about me, O God.
> They cannot be numbered!
> I can't even count them;
> they outnumber the grains of sand!
> And when I wake up,
> you are still with me!

PSALM 139:17-18

BIRTHDAY OF A FRIEND

———— • ————

FATHER OF EACH BIRTHDAY, I'm happy to celebrate the day my friend was born. You were there that day, God. You saw that her parents were out of their minds with excitement over the life you began nine months earlier and gave to them as a gift. Now an adult, my friend is a woman who sparkles, glows, and radiates your love to people around her. I feel rich for knowing her.

You describe your creative work in us as wonderfully complex, to which some around us might smile and say a hearty "Amen!" Whenever life feels especially complex to my friend, please help her remember that you always understand us—even on days we can't seem to understand ourselves.

Loving Maker, please help my friend remember that before she was born, every single moment of her life was known to you. You have been, you are, and you will continue to be with her each day. May she trust you to be her faithful guide. Your thoughts about each of us are precious, and they can't be numbered. Please help my friend to feel cherished in your sight.

Please satisfy her each day with your unfailing love, and bless her generously in the year ahead. Thank you, Father, for giving me such a special friend.

BLENDED FAMILIES

———•———

HEAVENLY FATHER, I come to you with blended families on my heart. Whether it's the blending of a treasured child with adoptive parents, a child who is being raised by either grandparents or a family friend, or second marriages combining new children or new spouses, blended families face all of the usual challenges of a family, plus a few extras.

Please give these friends wisdom and understanding, especially as each member of their family adjusts to new roles. May they relate to each other with patience and kindness, and speak the truth in love. Help them avoid passive or aggressive attitudes, choosing instead to discuss their feelings and concerns in respectful ways that honor each family member involved.

Please provide healing, over time, for unpleasant memories of the past that sometimes collide with things in the present. When they need fresh vision and helpful perspectives, please lead them to wise counselors. And Father, kindly knit their hearts together as only you can. For all this, we offer you great thanks.

BRIDAL SHOWER

———— • ————

FATHER GOD, as friends and family of this loving couple, we've gathered to celebrate their upcoming marriage. Thank you for designing marriage and for blessing this radiant bride and groom with the gift of each other. We're grateful for the heritage you've given them through their parents and grandparents.

We joyfully shower this couple with gifts today because we're eager to launch them on their way. In addition to the beautifully wrapped presents, we also offer our prayers on their behalf. Please nudge us to pray for them as they come to mind. Our prayers are gifts that keep on giving.

Please satisfy this husband and wife from the fountain of your unfailing love. Remind them how much you love them, and give them love to share with each other. When they face challenges in small, moderate, and large things—as all married couples do—may they run to you, ask for wisdom and help, and find you to be their strength and peace. Please help them look for ways to cherish one another every day.

Shine your face on this couple, Lord, and bless them with a fruitful and understanding marriage. In the name of Jesus, our faithful Lover.

BUSY DAY AT WORK

———— • ————

LORD, today will be a very busy day. Meetings are scheduled, problems need to be solved, and certain tasks must be completed. No doubt there will be interruptions, which sometimes throw me off balance. I haven't even begun working, and I feel overwhelmed just thinking about it all.

Lord, calm my spirit and relieve my anxiety so I can think clearly. Give me wisdom to perceive what's most important and perseverance to complete the projects I begin. You have always been there in the past. Many times, you have intervened and brought unexpected blessings out of difficult challenges. Help me to remember those blessings and to be a good and faithful servant today. Amen.

Work willingly at whatever you do, as though you were working for the Lord rather than for people. Remember that the Lord will give you an inheritance as your reward, and that the Master you are serving is Christ.

COLOSSIANS 3:23-24

CAREGIVER

— • —

KIND SHEPHERD, some of us find ourselves in a caregiving season. We tend to our elders, our peers, our children—and perhaps grandchildren—while trying to keep up with our own jobs and lives. Weariness is no stranger to us. At times, we feel like we're in a tug-of-war, and we wonder if we're being stretched to the limit!

During your three years of ministry on earth, you cared not only for the needs of those close to you, but also for crowds of strangers with a variety of issues. At the end of that time, you emptied yourself of everything but love. You cared about us enough to die for us. You sacrificed your last drops of blood for us in the ultimate caregiving moment. We can't thank you enough, Jesus.

Please help me order my time and use my energy well as I follow your example of serving those around me. May I never hesitate to give you my heavy burdens because you desire to assist me. Help me find time to quiet my heart and be restored by your Word.

CAREGIVING

——— • ———

COMPASSIONATE JESUS, whenever I read about your gentleness, tenderness, and compassion in the Bible, I'm deeply moved. You noticed a man with a deformed hand, and you restored it. You saw the hungry crowds, and you fed them. You touched a leper, and his leprosy disappeared. You gave sight to a blind man and revealed to him that you are the Son of God. What a kind and caring Savior you are! In this responsibility I am now undertaking, I need more of your gentle and kind ways, Lord.

In 1 Corinthians 12, you mention specific gifts you give to your children, all of them intended to help others. I'm grateful for the patient service of people who've helped my extended family. Thank you for bringing these people alongside us at just the right times.

Lord, as I care for the people around me who need help—whether it be a child, a person with special needs, or a loved one who is ill—please fill me with your strength and grace. May I treat the person I'm caring for in ways I would want to be treated if I were the one in need.

CHRISTENING

———— • ————

Father God, one of our friend's children will be baptized today in the tradition of her family's church. This is a significant and joyful time, as parents and friends commit themselves to bringing up this child to know you and love you. Please bless her parents, who have hopes and dreams for this newest member of their family. No one but you, Lord, knows the course of this child's life, so we entrust her to your unending love, care, and mercy.

May the seed of your Word take root in her heart, growing in fertile soil that is watered by Christ-followers around her. May older believers train her well in the ways of God and embed your Word in her heart. As you weave the events and circumstances of her life together, may it be a tapestry of beauty and grace.

May we remain engaged with this child's family, faithfully supporting, encouraging, and contributing good things to this dear one who is loved by you and all of us. In the name of the Father, Son, and Holy Spirit, amen.

And it came to pass in those days, that there went out a decree from Caesar Augustus, that all the world should be taxed. . . . And Joseph also went up from Galilee, out of the city of Nazareth, into Judaea, unto the city of David, which is called Bethlehem . . . to be taxed with Mary his espoused wife, being great with child. . . . And she brought forth her firstborn son, and wrapped him in swaddling clothes, and laid him in a manger; because there was no room for them in the inn.

LUKE 2:1, 4-5, 7, KJV

CHRISTMAS

———— • ————

LORD JESUS, the account of your birth in Scripture is so familiar, yet full of mystery and wonder. Year after year, I hear the story and ponder its meaning all over again. What a miracle! You—God—became man and were willing to walk beside us, leaving the glory of heaven to experience a humble life on earth.

This season is filled with activities and events that easily distract me from contemplating the true significance of Christmas. You are the most precious gift ever given to humankind. And yet, too often I leave you out in the cold, giving little thought to the monumental significance of your coming. Like those in Bethlehem, I can become so busy with other things that I don't find room in my heart for you.

Lord, I open my heart to you. I present myself to you as a dwelling place. It is only because of your mercy and forgiveness that my feeble temple is deemed worthy for you to reside in. I pray that others will see your presence in my life and be compelled to know you, not merely as a baby in a manger but as a life-giving Savior.

CHRONIC ILLNESS

———— • ————

CARING FATHER, I come to you boldly, asking you to encourage my friends who have chronic illnesses. Each has had more doctor appointments, lab tests, and hospital procedures than they or their families ever expected.

When I stop to ponder the burdens they carry, I am certain they sometimes feel overwhelmed—not just physically, but mentally, emotionally, and spiritually. Give me wisdom to know how to be a good friend.

Please hold my friends close, especially on days when they are discouraged and struggling to keep going. Please shield them from fear and give them a sense of purpose. For the medical staff supervising their care, please provide wisdom, attentiveness, and insight in liberal amounts. And please help those of us who are friends, cheerleaders, and caregivers to be warmhearted, sensitive, and loving.

Even though the chronic illnesses my friends live with affect their lives in significant ways, please prevent them—and those of us who love them—from allowing their illnesses to undermine their worth or define their personhood. We have so much to learn from their lives and their journeys.

Please, Father, lavish your love and compassion on my friends.

COMMUNION

——— • ———

GRACIOUS LORD, today, I plan to worship you by taking Communion in the fellowship of your people. As your children, we will remember the amazing sacrifice you made on our behalf. We will recall that horrible night when you were betrayed, when you broke bread and said to your disciples, "Take this and eat it, for this is my body." After giving bread to your disciples, you took a cup of wine and gave thanks to God for it. When you gave your disciples the cup, you said, "This is my blood, which confirms the covenant between God and his people. It is poured out as a sacrifice to forgive the sins of many."

Lord Jesus, as I take this bread and cup today, I remember what you have done for me. You willingly paid the ultimate price for my sin when you were nailed to a cross. None of my efforts were enough to make me right with you. It's because of your mercy that all my sins have been forgiven. I am in awe of what you have done for me. May I never forget the miracle of your love. Thank you, Jesus. Amen.

CONFIRMATION

———— • ————

DEAR LORD, my young friend is about to be confirmed in the church where he and his family are members. He has prepared for this day and has shown commitment to Christ and his church. He has affirmed his understanding of his church's doctrines and teachings, and his intentions to continue growing with this fellowship of believers.

Lord, I pray you would strengthen my friend's faith in you. Please bless him with wisdom, understanding, and good judgment. I ask that your Holy Spirit would fill him with courage, knowledge, and reverence. May he often glimpse your grace and glory. Surely, all of these things are gifts you willingly give to any of us. We acknowledge our need for these gifts, as well as for discipline to practice them in daily life.

Please guide my friend into truth, empower him to make a difference, and enable him to be loyal to you. May this child of yours live in union with you and be so filled with your Spirit that his life will be an inspiration and example to people around him. Please bless this future leader, Lord—today, and in all his years to come. Amen.

CRITICISM

———— • ————

GOD WHO KNOWS ALL THINGS, being criticized is not
a pleasant experience. In my discomfort, I'm thankful it's
safe to talk with you about my feelings. You know what's
happened and understand the situation much better than
I do.

Sometimes, I'm not quick to identify my feelings or
be honest about them—with myself, with others, or with
you. I need your help in sorting things out, God. Other
times, I lurch from one extreme to another. One minute
I beat myself up over what another person said about me,
and the next minute I feel like hurling a barb right back.

Father, please calm me. May I think carefully about
the criticism that's come my way, since there's often some
truth I can glean from it. You teach us in the book of
Proverbs that people who stubbornly refuse to accept
criticism will suddenly be destroyed beyond recovery.
I don't want that to happen. Nor do I want to wallow in
anger and self-pity, because it's very difficult to climb out
of those pits once I've jumped in.

Father, please help me work through this experience
in a healthy way, knowing that you are with me, you are
eager to help me grow, and you will strengthen me.

DEATH IN A FRIEND'S FAMILY

———— • ————

GOD WHO RECORDS ALL OUR DAYS, you know all about us, from the moment we receive the spark of life until we take our last breath. The last day came for my friend's father, Lord. All along, you've known the exact time and place this man's life would be completed. For us, though, the details surrounding a loved one's death usually come as a surprise.

Father, please comfort my friend and each of her family members in the days ahead, as they gather together from various parts of the country. Keep them safe as they travel, and spread your wings of protection over them. Thank you that you care for each of these people as individuals, since the way we humans process our grief and loss isn't one-size-fits-all.

Bless this extended family with your grace and love as they spend time talking, weeping, and laughing together over shared experiences and memories. Because no family is exempt from relational scrapes and wounds, I ask you to provide your liberal and tender healing wherever it's needed.

In the days ahead, may each one of them be reminded of your goodness and unfailing love, which pursue us every day of our lives.

DEDICATION OF A CHILD

—— • ——

FATHER GOD, this cherished child will soon be dedicated to you in front of a congregation of your people. Like Mary and Joseph, who carried the baby Jesus to be dedicated in the Temple, we ask you to bless this family and child.

Like Jesus' family, may this family be committed to following you throughout their lives. May your mercy, goodness, and blessing be theirs every day. Please protect them from evil and give them courage and resolve to do what is good. May your Spirit bestow his gifts on this child in abundance, and may he—like the young boy Jesus—obediently bend his will to those who are authorities in his life.

Through each stage of his life, may this child deepen his walk with you, so that his fellowship with you will be intimate and strong. And at the end of his days, may it be said that he was a light for Jesus in the world, reflecting your glory and demonstrating to everyone what it means to be a person who follows you. Amen.

DESPERATION

———— • ————

GOD OF HEAVEN, there are times in my life—and the lives of my family and friends—when I realize how very desperate I am for your help. Someone has received a cancer diagnosis. Someone's lost a job. Someone's experiencing a lengthy depression. Someone's feeling trapped in a situation with no clear resolution.

When we're desperate, we fear we're going to crumble. We feel as if we're in an emotional tsunami. Just about the time we seem to recover from one crashing wave, another one comes breaking over us. Sometimes we don't know how we will keep going.

Please be my refuge, God, and give me your help and strength. I can't muster up my own. Please send people to encourage me. Please send ministering servants—your angels—to protect me. Please settle my heart. May I take time to be still and remember that you are God. My eyes are on you, Father. Please provide me with whatever I need—in this hour and in the days ahead. I choose to depend on you, the only one in the whole world who is totally dependable.

I pray that God, the source of hope, will fill you completely with joy and peace because you trust in him. Then you will overflow with confident hope through the power of the Holy Spirit.

ROMANS 15:13

DIVORCE AND CHILDREN

— • —

ALL-KNOWING GOD, many children of all ages are affected by the painful realities of their parents' divorce. People around their parents often wish they could have done something to prevent the end of the marriage, but such wishes regarding other people's situations and choices are just that—wishes.

You know everything there is to know about these children we care about, and that brings us comfort. You love them more than we do! Thank you for helping us learn over time that the only person whose attitudes, choices, and behaviors we have control over is . . . ourselves. The longer we live with this understanding, God, the more we run to you with our concerns.

In your power, wisdom, and mercy, please bless these children every day with physical, spiritual, and emotional well-being. We plead with you to provide people around them who will show them your kindness and compassion. Throughout their days, please help them sense your great love for them. Please give them many glimpses of your truth and grace, and nudge them to run to you for comfort, strength, and guidance.

EASTER

——— • ———

CONQUERING LORD, today I celebrate Easter:
Resurrection Sunday. My heart is full of joy and hope
because of what this day represents. Easter signifies the
day that you, Light of all light, burst forth from the
tomb with incredible power, crushing sin and death. The
brightest lights and grandest music can't begin to capture
what you, the Sunrise from on High, did that day. What
a stunning turnaround from the darkest of Fridays we
remembered somberly two days ago. On *that* day, when
an immovable stone sealed the place where you were
laid, it seemed all hope was lost. But death and the grave
simply could not hold you.

I recall some dark days in my life when I wondered if
there would ever be light and hope again. Those were days
that tested my faith and perseverance. But Resurrection
Sunday, the exclamation point of the Good News,
reminded me that you have triumphed over sin and death.

On this magnificent day, I worship you—the Giver of
all life. The Giver of *new* life. Amen!

ELDERLY PARENT

———— • ————

ABBA, FATHER, my earthly father-in-law is now very old, and day by day the light of his life is flickering. He is deep in the winter of his years, with stooped shoulders, eyes that no longer see, and ears that barely hear. Others must care for his many needs these days.

He has trusted you for salvation, and he looks forward to the day he will see your face. He is a man who has followed your path. The way ahead of him is winding toward the dark valley of death; he is approaching his river Jordan. With his eyes of faith, he seems to sense the brilliance of the land beyond, a colorful land of beauty scented by the fragrance of true fellowship. It will someday be his home of complete Sabbath rest.

Lord, please give him unfaltering courage and fullness of hope when he approaches the river of final passing. May you carry him in your arms and fill him with joy at the prospect of seeing your face.

> Because I am righteous, I will see you.
> When I awake, I will see you face to face and
>   be satisfied.

PSALM 17:15

EXPECTANT MOTHER

---•---

CREATOR GOD, it's impossible for me to imagine the number of babies who've ever been conceived—all around the world, since the beginning of time. You alone know that vast number because you're the Author of life.

One of my young friends shared some sparkling news with me, a secret you knew even before she did. You're forming a little person inside her, Father. *My friend is pregnant!* What a surprising gift, after so many difficult years of longing and loss. My friend has prayed and waited for such a long time that she can barely contain her joy.

Soon, she may see an image of her growing baby through an ultrasound, God, but you see what is happening right now, moment by moment. Please place your hand of blessing on this young mother and the tiny life inside her. Thank you that we can trust you to help us through all our days.

> You made all the delicate, inner parts of my body
>   and knit me together in my mother's womb.
>
> PSALM 139:13

FATHER'S DAY

——— • ———

FATHER GOD, thank you for blessing me with a kind, patient, and generous father. I wish all children could have that experience. The older I get, the more I realize it's not true in all families. Some children—even in adult years—find it difficult to grasp *your* unfailing love, partly because of painful memories associated with their earthly fathers. Maybe one of the reasons I haven't struggled to appreciate your kindness, patience, and generosity is that I've observed those qualities in my earthly father.

Please bless all children everywhere who need your help and perspective to work through painful or non-existent memories of their fathers. Please provide them with men in their lives who are outstanding and caring father figures, whether they are relatives, friends, colleagues, or pastors.

For those of us whose fathers are still living, may we be quick to express appreciation and thanks to them in spoken or written words for the specific ways they have influenced our lives. As our fathers age, may we be generous with our time, care, and attention, which will honor them and honor you. Amen.

FORGIVENESS AND ITS BENEFITS

——— • ———

RIGHTEOUS FATHER, this side of heaven, we can't be perfect—though we sometimes try. The sting of sin will be painfully present as long as we're living on this earth. You tell us that all our righteousness is like filthy rags. Yet you are perfectly righteous, loving, and fair, dressed in garments that are regal and holy. Sometimes we attempt to design our own new clothes . . . until we come to see them for the rags they really are. When we ask you for forgiveness, trusting in Jesus' death and resurrection to give us new life, you embrace us as your children and give us fresh new wardrobes.

Your line of clothing dresses us with mercy, kindness, humility, gentleness, patience, forgiveness, love, peace, and thankfulness. Thank you for giving us these lasting benefits. May our hearts reflect who you are to those around us.

O Lord, you are so good, so ready to forgive, so full of unfailing love for all who ask for your help.

PSALM 86:5

FORGIVENESS FROM GOD

———— • ————

GRACIOUS AND FORGIVING GOD, you see my heart. You know I sometimes try to convince myself I haven't sinned, although the truth is that I am only fooling myself. I might blame others for things I have brought upon myself. Help me instead to admit my sin and turn my heart toward you, my loving Father and kind Shepherd.

Maybe there's something I wish I hadn't done. Maybe it's something I wish I *had* done. Thank you that I don't need to be mired in remorse or regret. When your Spirit lives in my heart, these instructive feelings can become part of a healthy sorrow that leads me away from sin and pushes me toward restoration with you.

You are a God of compassion and mercy, slow to get angry and filled with unfailing love. You have assured us that if we confess our sins to you, you are faithful and just to forgive us our sins and to cleanse us from all unrighteousness. Thank you, God, for this wonderful gift offered to us—to be cleansed from the inside out. You alone can do it.

FRIENDSHIP

——— • ———

DEAR LORD, friendship is a special gift that I sometimes take for granted. There are so many lonely people in the world, yet over the years you have blessed me with many friends. Some are acquaintances, while others I hold close to my heart. But each friendship is refreshing in its own way.

You've told us that your Son, Jesus, is a friend of sinners, and I am grateful for that distinction. I am a sinner, and I surely need the friendship of Jesus. He was human and lived on earth just like me, so he is able to understand what that is like. Yet he is very God of very God, and he offers to help me with his divine power. Lord, may my relationship with you be reflected in the way I live. May my words be full of kindness and truth. May I be a faithful, trustworthy friend—ready to listen, ready to serve, and ready to encourage. Thank you for *your* friendship, which is the most cherished friendship of all.

There is no greater love than to lay down one's life for one's friends.

JOHN 15:13

FRIENDSHIP AND GRATITUDE

———— • ————

LORD, yesterday I had lunch with a close friend I've known for many years. I treasure our rich and deep relationship. We are present for each other during happy times and sad times. We listen carefully to each other's concerns, ask thoughtful questions, and pray that your will be done with the requests we bring to you. Sometimes it's a while between the visits, but our ongoing prayers keep us connected until we can meet again. Each time, we immediately pick up where we left off, a hallmark of our bond.

Thank you for blessing me with such a relationship, Lord. Your Word teaches that a true friend sticks closer than a brother—a sibling. You have given me many "siblings" I consider dear friends. Better yet, I am privileged that you have called me your friend and your sibling. On the day you rose victorious from the grave, you said, "Go tell my brothers . . ." When I was born again, I was adopted into your family, and we now have the same Father God. Lord, thank you for my earthly friends and siblings. May I reflect your grace, truth, and kindness to each of them.

FRIENDSHIP WITH GOD

—— • ——

MY FRIEND AND MY GOD, early each morning I look
forward to spending time with you, probably for some
of the same reasons I enjoy spending time with my
husband. It doesn't matter what my husband and I are
doing—working together, riding in the car, or cleaning
up the kitchen after dinner. What's important is that
we're *together*.

That's how I feel about my time with you, God. I
want to be with you. My husband knows me better than
anyone else on earth, and he loves me in spite of it. But
you know me *completely*—better than I know myself. I'm
grateful that you love me with unfailing love, even though
you know all my sins, weaknesses, and faults.

Thank you for your Word, God. It's my lifeline,
and I don't know what I'd do without it. Thank you for
your Spirit, who helps me apply your truth and gives
me insight and guidance for everyday challenges. It's no
wonder I'm eager to spend time with you. May I never
take any of this for granted, Lord.

GOD DRAWS US

—— • ——

Loving God, thank you for drawing us to yourself through your world, your workmanship, and your Word.

You grab our attention with the sun and the moon, visible evidence of your magnificent creation from the very beginning. When I see a stunning sunset, it's *your* handiwork on display. When I rise in the wee hours of the morning and gaze at a full moon through the skylight, something in the recesses of my heart compels me to think of you. Thank you, Father, for such beauty.

You captivate us through your gift of physical life. Our bodies don't need to be plugged into an electrical outlet to be recharged; instead, your gifts of food and sleep keep us energized and going until the end of our days. We are your masterpieces, made in your image. When I stop to ponder how you've designed the parts of my body to work together, I'm drawn to you yet again.

You beckon us to you through your Word. It's a privilege to spend time reading it because its pages reveal who you are. The more we read about you, Father, the more we want to spend time with you.

GOD'S FAITHFULNESS

—— • ——

GENEROUS GOD, at times I'm slow to learn your ways and quick to forget how faithfully you provide—just as Jesus' disciples were. After witnessing Jesus perform the miracle of feeding five thousand people with five loaves of bread and two fish, then later feeding a crowd of four thousand from equally meager fare, the disciples were concerned when they forgot to pack food for themselves for the next part of the journey. So swiftly they forgot!

And yet my memory can be just as short. I see your hand in my life and delight in the ways you have sustained me, but days later, I toss and turn, worrying about new unresolved problems. I need to hear the echo of the words Jesus said to his disciples: "How many leftovers did you pick up afterward? Don't you understand yet?"

Lord, help me to remember how many times you have fulfilled my needs. Help me to get it! With you, my mighty God and Creator, there is no shortage of bread, no lack of resources. You have proclaimed to all of us, "I am the bread of life. Whoever comes to me will never be hungry again." Thank you, Father, for filling me up.

PRAYERS FOR SPECIFIC OCCASIONS

ᏀOD'S HELP

— • —

MIGHTY GOD, we need reinforcements. At times we feel attacked from various directions, and we wonder how we will ever defeat the adversaries intent on destroying us, from without and within. Though we're not fighting physical battles with weapons such as David was when he penned the words below, we are fighting real battles nonetheless.

Whether our situation seems like a squabble, a tug-of-war, or major combat, we need your wisdom, strength, and resources. You are our wisdom, Father. May we seek it in your Word and plead for it throughout the day. You are our strength, Father. We depend on you to give us vitality to do good and power to resist evil. You are the source of all help, Father, and you alone know what we need for the challenges we face. We gratefully acknowledge how you've helped us—and many others—in the past, and we humbly trust that you will take command and lead us to victory now.

Oh, please help us against our enemies,
　　for all human help is useless.
With God's help we will do mighty things,
　　for he will trample down our foes.

PSALM 60:11-12

GOD'S HELP FOR MY FRIEND

———— • ————

STRONG FATHER, I've seen your mighty power in many ways, and I believe nothing is impossible for you. I've read of the help you showed to people in ages past: to Joseph, Moses, Esther, David, Mary Magdalene, and many others in the Bible. Their stories have impacted my story.

I know that you still help people today, because you have helped me. You have intervened in numerous events of my life, and when I remember them, I am grateful all over again. I've also seen how you have transformed the lives of people I know, which has bolstered my faith in your resurrection power.

I come to you now, God, on behalf of a friend who needs to experience your unstoppable might and loving rescue. When she wishes she had wings of a dove and could fly far away, please send her strength and encouragement to persevere. When she feels so fearful that she can't stop shaking, please calm her heart. When she feels overwhelmed, please give her abundant support.

Thank you that we can hand you our burdens and know that you care for us. Please show your loving care to my friend today, Lord.

In the strong name of Jesus, amen.

GOD'S INVITATION

——— • ———

FATHER, you've made our hearts, and yet, curiously, you don't come barging in to take over. You stand outside, you knock, and you wait for us to invite you in. You promise that when we hear you, respond to you, and open the door, you will come in and visit with us, as a friend.

My heart quickens when I ponder this. It's stunning to think that you—the God who created the world, who sent your Son to earth to die for the sins of the world, and who gave Jesus a seat at your right hand in heaven— would care enough about me to want to pursue a relationship. And yet you do.

Thank you for coming into my heart, kind Father. The time I spend with you is not just sitting down to an ordinary meal. It's a lavish feast!

Look! I stand at the door and knock. If you hear my voice and open the door, I will come in, and we will share a meal together as friends.

REVELATION 3:20

GOD'S JEALOUS
LOVE FOR US

——— • ———

LOVING GOD, can you *really* be jealous over us—over me?
How can this be?

Psalm 78:58 recounts that the Israelites "angered God
by building shrines to other gods; they made him jealous
with their idols." I've read this verse before, but I must
have glossed over the part about your children making
you jealous with their idols. As I let these words sink into
my mind, I am humbled that you would react that way.
I feel loved and treasured to think that you would be jealous over us—over me.

I also feel sad when I reflect on times in my life
when I've turned to other things instead of turning to
you. Please accept my confession and forgive me, Father.
May this picture of your jealous love shape the thoughts,
choices, and decisions I make throughout each day. I don't
want to choose other things instead of you.

Thank you, Father, for allowing me to catch a glimpse
of how much you love me.

GOD'S WONDERS

——— • ———

LORD, you've done wonderful things in the past and you're doing wonderful things now. Sometimes it's easy for me to notice the work of your hands, such as when I visit the Grand Canyon. Or when I hold a newborn baby and marvel at your plan to keep humankind going. Or when I step into a flower shop and catch the sweet fragrance of gardenias.

Other times—when things in my life aren't going well—I'm not so quick to see your wonders. During those times, I'm especially grateful for your Word. As I read it, I'm reminded of those who have come before me, many of whom were in dire situations, yet trusted you and lived to see wonders they couldn't have imagined. Moses witnessed the horrible Egyptian plagues, yet he saw you part the waters of the Red Sea. Hannah was childless, yet she eventually experienced the thrill of bearing and raising several children. Jesus' followers witnessed his gruesome death on the cross, yet they were visited by Jesus after he rose from the dead. Then he blessed them with the presence of the Holy Spirit.

God, please give me grace to trust you, whether I'm seeing your wonders now . . . or waiting for some yet to come.

GOOD FRIDAY

———— • ————

DEAR LORD JESUS, today we remember the darkest of all days—Good Friday. The events that occurred two millennia ago hardly qualify as good, until we put them in context. Only when we consider what those horrors ultimately achieved for us—our salvation—can we call them good, supremely good. You, the Lord and Master of all things, were betrayed and brutalized by people you created. They despised you for rewriting their rules and expectations, and they mercilessly took your life—killing you, the Giver of all life! They did it out of jealous greed, terrible ignorance, and despicable motives, and they represent all of us. We can scarcely grasp the agony of your death. That Friday was so dark that even the sun hid in deep grief.

Jesus, we are grateful—exceedingly grateful—that your story did not end on that darkest of days. Even as we somberly remember what happened, we know what took place three days later. You arose with blazing light and glory as you conquered our worst enemy—death itself. Light of light, true God from true God—you did it for us! We want to honor you and give you thanks. Amen.

GRADUATION

—— • ——

LORD OF OUR LIVES, this is a special day for my child—
graduation day! Since before he was born, we have antici-
pated the day he would be launched into adulthood. We
have spent these years doing our best to support him
in his interests, endeavors, school, and activities, all the
while watching and wondering what he might pursue.
Even on this day, we don't know what the sum of his
life will be. But you do, Lord; you love this child of ours
more than we do. You know him intimately and have
wonderful plans for him. May he choose to love you with
all his heart, soul, mind, and strength. Please protect
him, give him wisdom, and grant him success. May he
hold on to the truth that you have been sustaining his life
from day one.

> You watched me as I was being formed in utter
>   seclusion,
>   as I was woven together in the dark of the womb.
> You saw me before I was born.
>   Every day of my life was recorded in your book.
> Every moment was laid out
>   before a single day had passed.
>
> PSALM 139:15-16

GRANDDAUGHTER

---•---

FATHER, I'll never forget the day my granddaughter was born. You graced her face with two cute dimples and gave her beautiful dark hair and eyes. I was *thrilled* to have a granddaughter, God! After having three sons and no daughters, this was my chance to think pink. I didn't waste any time; I baked sugar cookies and decorated them with pink icing.

My granddaughter is growing up, Father. No longer a toddler, she's going to school now. Bless her with good friends, and may they encourage one another to make wholesome choices.

Thank you that my granddaughter is kind, a virtue you encourage us to "write deep within our hearts." Please draw her tender heart toward you and help her to understand how deep and wide your love is. As she hears your Word, may it take root in her heart, tasting sweet now and sweeter still in the years to come.

Please protect her body, mind, and spirit, and guide her, Good Shepherd of her heart. May she grow in godliness and inner beauty, and realize how very precious she is to you.

GRANDPARENTS

—— • ——

GOD, MY FATHER, you are the original Father. You have no father or grandfather, for you have always existed and have not descended from anyone. Existing from time immemorial, you are the great I AM. We have all descended from Adam and Eve, your first created couple—person after person, family after family, generation after generation.

You blessed me with grandparents who loved you. Although it has been years since they left this world to claim their home with you, I am the recipient of that godly legacy. Lord, accept my thanks for the good things—both material and spiritual—you passed on to me through my parents and grandparents. I'm grateful for shared experiences and treasured memories that through the corridors of time still reverberate messages of love to me.

Now I have the privilege of being a grandparent.

Teach me how to be a gracious and godly grandparent. I want to pass good things to future generations. May I be faithful in declaring your goodness and kindness in word and deed. Please help me to be an accurate reflection of your grace, your truth, and your love. Amen.

GRANDSON

———— • ————

DEAR FATHER, you have blessed my husband and me with a delightful grandson! Shortly after he was born, we held him in our arms, cradling this new heir from a new generation. We watched him move, marveled at his handsome features, and wondered at the potential in his little life. What joy!

Years have gone by. As our grandson's character has developed, we've enjoyed his curiosity and sense of humor, learned what he likes and dislikes, and made lots of memories with him. It has been great fun to see his life unfold.

At times when we've smiled at his mischievous antics, we've been reminded of our own. How we need you to guide and direct us all—grandparents, children, and grandchildren alike.

Thank you for the gifts and abilities you've given our grandson, Lord. We're grateful that he loves you and loves your Word. Already, we catch glimpses of a future leader. Please help us to nurture and encourage him, Father. May this young grandson of ours develop a rock-solid faith. Like Jesus, may he grow in wisdom and stature, and in favor with God and people. Amen.

GRIEF

— • —

GRACIOUS FATHER, many of us have felt some measure of grief in our lives. No matter its source or its duration, grief is not a welcome visitor to anyone.

That was surely the case, Father, for young Joseph in the Old Testament. The apple of his father's eye, Joseph had no idea that he would be betrayed by his brothers, enslaved and imprisoned, and then separated from his family and country for what seemed like forever.

Thank you, Father, for Joseph's story in the Bible. I weep whenever I read it. At first, my tears flow from deep sadness that Joseph endured so much anguish and loss. But when the story takes a turn—when Joseph rises to success and is reunited with his grieving father who thought his son had been dead all those years—my tears spring from pure joy!

O God, in Joseph's grief we feel our own grief. May we see that you are *with us* in our suffering too. May we understand that even when others intend harm, you intend good and can overrule evil to accomplish your perfect plans. With your help, Father, we can each become fruitful in the land of our grief.

HEALING

— • —

Dear Jesus, my friend is very ill. Her sickness has persisted for some years now, each time returning with a new vengeance that ravages her body. Doctors blessed with knowledge and expertise have been attending her, yet the treatments have drained her nearly as much as the disease itself. It is very difficult for her friends and family to see her struggle. Many of us have prayed for her healing, yet day by day she seems no better.

You touched and healed many people while you lived on this earth—the blind, the crippled, and those troubled by demonic activity, among others. You even raised some people from the dead! Everywhere you went, you brought healing, life, and joy—affirming that everything is possible with you. And yet not everyone was healed. Some people did not cross your path, were not touched, and continued to suffer with their conditions.

For my friend, I pray for healing and hope, and most of all, for unwavering faith. Please assure her that even in the midst of difficult days, you have not abandoned her, and you are in control. Please, Jesus, show my friend your continuous love in special ways.

HEALING AND FAITH

———— • ————

KIND JESUS, when a desperate synagogue leader named Jairus fell at your feet and pleaded for you to come heal his dying daughter, you went with him. On the way there, Jairus received news that his daughter was already dead, but you said, "Don't be afraid. Just have faith."

When you arrived at the house, people waiting outside laughed at you when you said the little girl wasn't dead. And yet you, your disciples, Jairus, and his wife went right to the little girl's room. You simply said, "Little girl, get up!" And she did. Immediately. Oh, the joy!

Jairus and his family were amazed at your power, and so are we. In our desperate times, Jesus, we turn to you too. Where else would we go? You alone are the way, the truth, and the life.

Like Jairus, we beg for your presence. We want you to come with us. Thank you that you went with Jairus and that you promise to go with us. Like Jairus, may we listen to you and heed your gentle words: "Don't be afraid. Just have faith." Oh, how we long for your healing touch in our lives and in our families.

HEALING POWER

—— • ——

LORD JESUS, when you healed a blind man from
Bethsaida, you didn't do it all at once. You healed him
in stages. At first, this puzzled me. You spit on the man's
eyes, which seems strangely disrespectful. Then you asked
the man if he could see. Of course you already knew his
answer, which was something like "Not exactly." The
man's vision was blurry; to him, people looked like trees
walking around. That's not a full healing, Jesus. But then
you touched him, and the miracle was complete.

I'm reminded of another incident of spitting detailed
in your Word, but this time *you* were being spit upon
in contempt. Yet this was part of the way in which you
brought ultimate healing to all of us. By your wounds,
we are healed.

Thank you for your healing power, Lord. We would
be hopeless without it. Help us to trust you as we wait for
your unique ways of renewing, rebuilding, and renovating
our hearts. You alone can make us whole.

Whatever is in your heart
determines what you say.
A good person produces good
things from the treasury of
a good heart, and an evil person
produces evil things from the
treasury of an evil heart.
And I tell you this, you must give
an account on judgment day for
every idle word you speak.

MATTHEW 12:34-36

A Heart after God

O God, I need your help with my heart, since what is in my heart determines what comes out of my mouth.

Jesus said that a person's heart is like a *treasury*—a personalized museum of sorts. Father, you know what each room and hallway of my heart looks like. You know exactly what is stored there; the contents often spill out through my words and actions.

In Galatians 5 the apostle Paul points out potential sins we might keep hidden away: sexual immorality, impurity, lustful pleasures, idolatry, sorcery, hostility, quarreling, jealousy, outbursts of anger, selfish ambition, dissension, division, envy, drunkenness, and wild living. Those kinds of things are dishonoring to you, destructive to us, and hurtful to people around us. Instead, I want my life to be filled with your love, joy, peace, patience, kindness, goodness, faithfulness, gentleness, and self-control. Cleanse my heart so I will be ready to receive the Holy Spirit's gifts.

As I turn my heart to you and your Word, Father, please help me to be a good curator of this treasury!

HEAVEN

— • —

Lᴏʀᴅ Gᴏᴅ ᴏꜰ Hᴇᴀᴠᴇɴ'ꜱ Aʀᴍɪᴇꜱ, how is it that you can live in heaven and in my heart at the same time? I don't understand how that works, but I'm grateful.

If I were to tour a royal palace somewhere in the world, I might think of you and your heavenly Kingdom. An ornate throne used by monarchs over the centuries might make me wonder what your throne looks like. As I walk through a grand hall that could easily seat hundreds of people, I might wonder what the capacity of your banquet hall in heaven will be. When studying the details of a royal scepter on display, I might remember that your authority is perfectly righteous and just, not cruel or capricious like worldly kingdoms that rise and fall.

To think that I can speak to you, the ultimate King of kings, at any hour of the day or night is overwhelming. Mighty God, I am in awe that you listen to my requests. In those moments when I wonder what it would be like to be related to royalty, I realize that through faith in Jesus, I am—now and forever!

HONESTY

—— • ——

FATHER, I need your help today to choose honesty and goodness in everything I do and say. When I'm tempted to shade the truth, I want to immediately say, "I'm slipping, God! Help me do the honest thing in this situation." You're always ready to assist. I just need to ask.

Dishonesty causes so much pain in our lives, God. All of us have been on the receiving end of deceitfulness, and sadly, we've all been on the giving end too. If we tell a lie, the person we dupe will eventually feel marginalized, put at a disadvantage, or even hated by us. You tell us in Proverbs that "a lying tongue hates its victims." That's sobering, God.

Please help me to be honest with myself, honest with you, and honest with others. May I keep learning how to speak the truth in love.

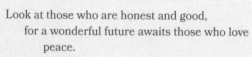

Look at those who are honest and good,
    for a wonderful future awaits those who love
        peace.
PSALM 37:37

JESUS' LOVE

———— • ————

TENDER JESUS, thank you that although we may some-times feel that we are an inconvenience to people around us, we are *never* an inconvenience to you.

Many years ago, your disciples were leaving Jericho with you. When two blind men heard that you would be passing by, they began shouting, "Lord, Son of David, have mercy on us!" But when the crowd around the two men yelled for them to be quiet, the two only yelled louder.

I love what you did next. You stopped and asked the blind men what they wanted you to do for them. When they answered, "We want to see!" you felt sorry for them, touched their eyes, and gave them sight. *And the men followed you.*

What hope and comfort these words bring us today. Regardless of what others around us think or how they treat us, we are *never* a bother to you. Quite the oppo-site! You stop for us, you listen to us, you feel for us, and you help us. What a wonderful helper and Savior you are, offering compassionate care. Our natural and loving response is to follow you.

JOB CHANGE

— • —

GOD OF NEW BEGINNINGS, many of us don't keep the same job for all of our working years, and we might face the looming challenge of finding a new job at some point. That's where one of my friends is now, God. I'm grateful you know my friend inside and out. You know her gifts. You know her family's needs. You know exactly where you are leading her . . . even though she doesn't have a clue at the moment.

In the Bible, we read about people from different walks of life to whom you assigned various tasks. At the time, they probably didn't realize how significant your guidance was. But we grasp its importance.

Father, for all who are involved in a job search, we ask for your protection while we hold fast to your promise.

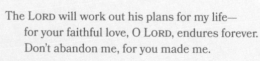

The LORD will work out his plans for my life—
for your faithful love, O LORD, endures forever.
Don't abandon me, for you made me.

PSALM 138:8

JOB SATISFACTION

—— • ——

SOVEREIGN GOD, as I reflect on my career, I'm grateful you've given me fulfilling employment over the years. Not only have you provided me with meaningful work, but that work has helped provide for my family and made it possible for us to help others. How generous you are!

Of course, there have been conflicts and challenges on the job, and sometimes I've been guilty of complaining. Yet in retrospect, I see how you have used those situations to grow me. On days I'm tempted to grumble, help me to remember your faithfulness.

Looking back over the zigs and zags of my life, I've had glimpses of how you've led me from one point to the next. I can't thank you enough for your kindness. For those I know who struggle in their jobs, please come alongside them and help them. You have certainly done that for me.

Each day as I begin my work, Father, may I represent you in everything I do.

JOB SEARCH

——— • ———

LORD JESUS, GIVER OF ALL GOOD GIFTS, several people in my circle of friends are presently out of work and fighting discouragement. The uncertainty of the future feels unsettling to them, and they are even beginning to question their personal worth and usefulness to their family and to society. I feel for these friends, and I lift them up to you.

Dear Jesus, please come close to my friends and their families today. Reassure them of your constant care, and remind them of ways you have faithfully provided for them in the past. May you strengthen their faith and provide even more than their expressed requests, now and in the days ahead. Amen.

> Don't worry about these things, saying, "What will we eat? What will we drink? What will we wear?" These things dominate the thoughts of unbelievers, but your heavenly Father already knows all your needs. Seek the Kingdom of God above all else, and live righteously, and he will give you everything you need. So don't worry about tomorrow, for tomorrow will bring its own worries. Today's trouble is enough for today.
> MATTHEW 6:31-34

LISTENING TO GOD

———— • ————

WONDERFUL TEACHER, when you lived on earth and trained your followers, you frequently started your lessons by saying, "Listen!" You used stories to make your point and applied those stories to your followers' lives. At times, you concluded by saying, "Anyone with ears to hear should listen and understand."

Throughout the course of my life you have been speaking to me, too. Sometimes it's been through circumstances, sometimes through people, and always through your Word. You have been showing me how your ways are better and higher than mine. Occasionally, my ears have been slow to hear and you have used pain to get my attention. Other times, your Spirit has opened my heart by gently guiding me—showing me how to improve, giving me hope for the future, and even helping me laugh at myself. Thank you for teaching me your ways without ever giving up on me. Thank you for your Word and your Spirit to instruct, confront, and comfort me. May I be quick to hear, slow to speak, and eager to learn—an attentive listener.

MARRIAGE CHALLENGES

———— • ————

GRACIOUS GOD, I'm feeling sad for a friend who's struggling in a difficult marriage. Even the best of marriages include challenging times, Lord. You've helped many of us move through troubles of various sorts, and over time, to emerge and experience pleasant days we wouldn't previously have imagined. With your help, nothing is impossible.

And yet my friend's situation is more serious than a minor disagreement. Father, in the days ahead, please encourage and strengthen her. Through your Word, through counselors, and through family and friends, please help her to know when it's wise to wait, and when it's important to act.

May she grow in learning to speak the truth in love, and in practicing the wise words of Romans 12:9: "Love must be sincere. Hate what is evil; cling to what is good" (NIV). It's challenging to know exactly what that looks like—practically speaking—from one minute to the next. But your Holy Spirit is a wonderful Counselor! Please be that for my friend in her situation, Lord. May she be heartened by the specific insights you provide. I ask this in the powerful name of Jesus, amen.

MARRIAGE IN CRISIS

— • —

MY SAVIOR, MY ROCK, I'm praying for a friend who's facing great turmoil in her marriage. Her husband has had repeated issues with destructive behaviors, and after much help from counselors and pastors, my friend has informed her husband she will no longer tolerate his addictions— his slavery to sin.

Father, this is a crucial time for this wife and her husband, and for their children. No doubt my friend is wondering how she can possibly have a healthy and loving marriage after what's been happening, and her husband might be wondering how he can possibly break free of his bondage to sin for the long haul.

I've seen people transformed, God. I *know* you can do exceedingly abundantly above all we ask or think. I also realize no one can be forced to turn to you for help. Give this husband resolve to take radical measures to move toward you and away from his addictions. Give this wife fortitude and wisdom for the challenges and decisions of each day. Help them both to see and deal with their contributions to this conflict. Please protect and bless their children, Father, in ways that you alone can. Please give each of them the help they need. I pray this in the victorious name of Jesus, amen.

MARRIAGE RESTORED

———— • ————

LOVING GOD, last night a friend described the joy of restating her marriage vows in a special ceremony at church. What satisfaction this brought to her and her husband, and what happiness I feel for them. My friend sensed your presence in the room, blessing her and her husband in a deep way. I'm grateful for signs of healing in the lives of these two children of yours.

They have climbed a long, difficult road. Years of betrayal, bitterness, and arguing were followed by the help of wise counselors, friends, and family. Week by week and month by month, they experienced advances—along with some setbacks—on their journey toward wholeness and trust.

I rejoice in your power to help them. Thank you for doing what seemed humanly impossible. You brought life to their marriage when it appeared to be dead. This shouldn't surprise me, Father, because you are a God who can raise the dead!

MARRIAGE REVITALIZED

———— • ————

FATHER, I know your Word has incredible power, because the following verses from Psalm 90 brought life-changing hope to my husband and me at a time when we desperately needed it. We were struggling to find encouragement and vision, and you graciously provided both. For many years now, you've listened to us pray the psalmist's words each morning, and we don't plan to stop.

I'm grateful you have upheld us with your steadfast love. We embrace the promises in this psalm because we have personally experienced them. Thank you for demonstrating how much you care for us. Our lives have not been trouble-free, but you have balanced the difficult times with the good ones.

You have kindly given us glimpses of your glory and power in our lives and in our friends' and family's lives. We are blessed to witness the expansion of your Kingdom in so many parts of your world. I thank you for all of this in the strong name of Jesus, amen.

Satisfy us each morning with your
unfailing love,
so we may sing for joy to the end
of our lives.
Give us gladness in proportion to
our former misery!
Replace the evil years with good.
Let us, your servants, see you
work again;
let our children see your glory.
And may the Lord our God show
us his approval
and make our efforts successful.
Yes, make our efforts successful!

PSALM 90:14-17

MEALTIME

———— • ————

Jesus, on busy days, preparing a meal for my family seems challenging. Figuring out how to feed a multitude of five thousand hungry people would be totally overwhelming. You did it, though, with only five loaves of bread and a couple of fish. Your miracle of multiplying one person's lunch into a bountiful feast was amazing. Maybe even more amazing was that you—the Bread of Life—took time to thank God the Father for the food.

I realize that some of us grew up in homes where a blessing was said before every meal; praying came naturally and even became somewhat routine as we used the same words over and over. Others of us have rarely prayed; we are uncomfortable talking to you or struggle to find appropriate words. But you, Jesus, have demonstrated that our prayers don't need to be eloquent. We can simply offer thanks for the food set before us, the people around us, and the ways you care for us. You are more concerned about our being grateful than about our finding the "perfect" words. What matters to you is what's in our hearts.

Your example of giving thanks encourages us to do it too. Thank you for providing for us, day after day. Amen.

MILITARY PERSONNEL

———— • ————

LORD OF HEAVEN'S ARMIES, you alone are the one true Conqueror, and the authority of all governments comes from you. In the end, it is your will and might that will triumph over the evil we see around us. Yet you have chosen to establish leaders, with their officers and military, to oversee countries throughout the world. You have commanded us to give honor and respect to those in power.

Please bless and protect the officers and enlisted men and women of our military forces, who faithfully serve our country. Some of these dedicated people are my family and friends, Lord. Please give all of them wisdom, righteousness, and honor. May they stand for what is just, fair, and good, even if others may not act or believe that way. Please surround our military people with your strength, and encourage them with your Word and your Spirit. For those who have suffered severe injuries or lost their lives to defend our freedom, we are immensely grateful. Father, please bring hope and healing to the injured, and comfort to the families and friends of those who have paid the ultimate price for our freedom. May all who serve be aware of your presence, and experience your abiding love in special ways. We ask this in the name of our Lord and King, Jesus. Amen.

MISCARRIAGE

—— • ——

FATHER, you know how very sad I feel today. I learned that a friend who was four months pregnant lost her baby. When I heard my friend's grievous news, my knees buckled and my heart ached. It's dawning on me that instead of my friend having a baby to lovingly cuddle in her arms, she has a raw, aching hole in her heart.

I beg you to lavish your comfort on my friend in ways that she knows come straight from you. God, I don't understand *how* your comfort works, but I know for certain that it does. You've comforted me before, and your presence was palpable. May my friend feel your tender presence, Lord. Though nothing will take away the pain she feels in her heart right now, please help her to realize your love as well as the love and care of family and friends. Please help those of us around her to avoid saying anything that would either downplay her pain or add to it. Help us to support her and be there for her. I pray all of this in the tender name of Jesus, amen.

MORNING PRAYER
FOR FAMILY

———— • ————

LOVING FATHER, thank you for blessing my family with children, who are gifts to be treasured. May I never lose my awe of your generosity.

As I've been reading the Old Testament book of Job, I was struck by something Job did: He offered you burnt offerings in the morning for each of his children. What are you trying to teach me through Job's act, Father? Even though Job followed you, he was human and had to deal with his sin problem. He obviously cared about his children and their sin issues too. By making special offerings to you for his children, maybe he was demonstrating his hopes that you would deal lovingly with his children's sins too. I get that, Lord. I have the same hopes for myself and for my children.

In that spirit, I offer you a prayer this morning that you will protect each member of my family and draw us all to yourself. May we see our need for you, experience your abundant love and forgiveness, and respond with a desire to spend time with you. I long to see these things in all our lives. In the strong name of Jesus, amen.

MOTHER'S DAY

———— • ————

LOVING GOD, when you sent your only Son to live among us as God in the flesh, you chose Mary's womb to be Jesus' first dwelling place. What an amazing plan, Father, and what an incredible way to elevate the role of motherhood. Though our yearly celebration of Mother's Day isn't something you instituted, you alone formed all the children that grew inside every mother who's ever lived. Which would include each of us and our mothers!

None of us have had perfect mothers, nor can any woman *be* a perfect mother. Yet you have asked all of us to *honor* our mothers. May we honor them with kindness and treat them with respect. Whether our mothers are close, far away, or just a memory, please help us to remember the varied ways they have contributed to our lives. As we send a card, make a phone call, extend an invitation, or pause to remember them, help us do it with a grateful spirit.

Some of us will celebrate Mother's Day as a child, some of us will celebrate as mothers, and some of us will celebrate as both. However we spend this special day, Father, may we realize that in honoring our mothers, we are also honoring you.

MOVING

—— • ——

GRACIOUS FATHER, this is an emotional day for me, one I wish were not here. My dear friend is moving away, and I'm heartbroken to see her go.

My friend's belongings are packed. She'll soon be leaving, and it's time for us to say good-bye. Please come alongside this one who is so dear to me as she leaves familiar relationships and surroundings—not knowing exactly what her life will be like in the new location. I'm grateful my friend has a relationship with you, Father, because I know your presence will go with her.

When she arrives at her new home, please give her stamina as she unpacks boxes, makes lots of decisions, and gets things situated. All of these things are exhausting. Please provide people on the other end who will offer help, kindness, and understanding. On days when things feel overwhelming, please help her to turn to you. May she be assured that you will bend down and listen as she expresses her feelings, needs, and concerns to you. Please bless her, helping her to grow and flourish in her new setting. May my friend's new home be a place of peace for her, for her family, and for all who visit.

NATIONAL LEADERS

——— • ———

SOVEREIGN GOD, you are the ruler of all nations and all people. No king, prime minister, president, or other authority governs without your consent. History is full of both good and evil rulers, and that is the reality of our nation's legacy too. Thank you for leaders of the past who submitted to your will, people who valued justice, mercy, and service as their high calling.

Lord, I pray for those who lead our nation today. May they guide with wisdom, understanding, care, and humility. Move in their hearts in ways that only you can. Give them a desire to serve, fortitude to stay true and honest, and wisdom to gather knowledgeable advisers around them. Remind us of our duty to pray for and submit to these authorities, even when we do not agree with their beliefs and policies. Should times come when we must obey you rather than our rulers, give us courage to stand up and wise words to speak. You have promised to give us your help in such times.

May our nation flourish under godly leadership that only you can provide. In Jesus' name, amen.

NEIGHBORS AND
COMMUNITY

———— • ————

Θ LORD, you have given us a wonderful community to live in, full of good neighbors. Our street is lined with beautiful trees, tidy houses, and the creative efforts of those surrounding us. Over the years we've all experienced the ups and downs of life—the joys of good times and the sorrows of troubles. In all of this, we enjoy being a part of this neighborhood.

Lord, bless this place we call home. May you shield and protect us from dangers that would harm or destroy us or our properties. Please prosper us in our work, equip us in our responsibilities, and enrich our families with growing relationships. May we walk in wisdom and seek you each day, so that in all of life you will be honored. Kindly help us to serve others in our community. May our home shine with your goodness and provide light to those who need to find their way. May we be an encouragement to all, demonstrating your mercy and enduring love. For the sake of your honor and your name, amen.

NEW HOME

———— • ————

GRACIOUS GOD, some of our friends are moving into their new home. This is a time of excitement and joy as they anticipate new beginnings. Fresh activities, memories, and cycles of life will unfold there. Times of planning, work, leisure, and rest lie before them, with so many hopes and dreams to realize.

Lord, I pray your best for our friends in the months and years ahead. Give them special favor and prosperity in this new place. Please protect them, and fill them with joy. May this be a haven of safety, peace, and growth for each member of their family. May your Word be treasured, taught, and followed, and may all who enter their home sense your undeniable presence there.

May the LORD bless you
    and protect you.
May the LORD smile on you
    and be gracious to you.
May the LORD show you his favor
    and give you his peace.

NUMBERS 6:24-26

NOTHING IS
IMPOSSIBLE WITH GOD

——— • ———

GREAT PHYSICIAN OF BODY, SOUL, AND MIND, my heart quickens whenever I read the account of how you healed a man with advanced leprosy. The deformed man presented you with a huge request. He needed you to do something that seemed impossible. I identify with that man; I can stand right alongside him. I'm aware of circumstances in my life and in my family's and friends' lives that seem impossible too.

I love how the man with leprosy approached you. When he saw you, he bowed down with his face to the ground and begged you to heal him. He said, "Lord, if you are willing, you can heal me and make me clean."

The way you responded to him, Lord, was beautifully tender. You reached out, touched the leprous man, and said, "I am willing. Be healed!" And instantly, he *was*.

I want my posture and attitude to be like the man in this story, Lord Jesus. I want to approach you reverently and directly with things that seem impossible to me and to the people around me. Thank you that with you, all things are possible.

ORDINATION TO MINISTRY

·

DEAR LORD, today is a special day for my friend who will be ordained to the ministry. I'm thankful he has completed his journey of formal training and qualification by a wise group of ministerial leaders. Most important, I'm moved that he is willing to serve your people in this sacred way. This is a unique and holy calling, and my friend is being set apart to do your work, as your servant.

Although we are celebrating this occasion today, it signifies the beginning of a lifetime of service to you, God, and to your church. Some days will be joyful and happy, while others will include difficulties and discouragement. I pray, Lord, that you would equip and strengthen my friend to faithfully fulfill your calling. Grant him discernment, fortitude, and humility. Please guide him in your ways and cause him to be a great source of encouragement, hope, and knowledge to the people in his care.

Ordination is a calling that no one can take on by themselves. So I pray that you would equip my friend for all the good work that you have planned in advance for him to do. For the sake of your Son, Jesus Christ, amen.

PALM SUNDAY

——— • ———

PRAISE YOU, KING JESUS! In my mind's eye, I can
picture you gently mounting the donkey colt you rode
into Jerusalem on the first Palm Sunday. The donkey
carried you up the winding roadway, with crowds of
cheering supporters laying down their coats and strewing
palm branches along the way. There was such excitement,
enthusiasm, and adoration. But you knew what lay ahead,
Jesus. Later, you wept over the people of Jerusalem who
didn't understand the way to peace. You knew how fickle
this crowd of people really was. Far into the future you
could see all of us—including me—joyfully worshiping
you one day, and then denying you a few days later.

Lord Jesus, give me the steadiness to worship you not
just in the midst of a supportive crowd, but day in and
day out. Not just in public worship, but in the quietness
of my home, and when I am alone in my thoughts. May
I worship you not just in a parade of honor, but in all of
life's ordinary moments—in good times and bad times, in
joy and in sorrow. For you are the Lord of all things. You
are my King and my God. Hosanna!

PARENTS AND GRANDPARENTS

—— • ——

MERCIFUL AND FAITHFUL FATHER, I'm grateful you've blessed me with children and grandchildren. My life is continually enriched because of them. Yet sometimes, I am deeply concerned for them, shedding tears over difficult situations I wish I could change or control . . . but I can't. I'm thankful I can pray, and I'm thankful that you listen. Where else would I go, Lord?

At times, anxiety for my children and grandchildren gets tangled up with disappointments over my own flawed parenting or grandparenting skills. I made mistakes, Lord, as every parent except you does. Help me not to be mired in painful regrets. Even you—the only perfect parent in the world—lamented that the children you raised and cared for had rebelled. It's comforting for me to realize that you completely understand my situation. More than that, you have power to help!

That is why I am praying, God. Please grant me discernment and wisdom. Sometimes it's challenging to know the difference between helping and hurting. But I know that your Spirit is willing to guide me. I have so much yet to learn. I'm depending on your Spirit to guide me.

PARENTS OF A PRODIGAL

———— • ————

GRACIOUS FATHER, it's happened on two occasions in church during a song. Each time I was sitting close to a married couple who walk with you, both concerned about an adult child of theirs who has wandered far from you.

The first time, I noticed that the father in front of me broke down at the words of a song about the biblical Prodigal Son returning home to his father. My friend began to silently weep, his shoulders and arms shaking with emotion. Comfort him, Father.

The second time, the song "Softly and Tenderly" was being sung. The words describe your Son Jesus' loving call to each of us wanderers—a call to come home, to rest from the weariness of life, to choose a rich and satisfying life with Jesus. I could see the hurting couple next to me wiping their eyes. Be close to them, Father.

Please encourage the longing hearts of these parents and countless others like them. Give them love and patience as they wait, pray, and hope. I plead with you to bring your followers—people infused with your Spirit, people who will reflect your great mercy and love—into the lives of these children, graciously pointing these dearly loved sojourners back to you.

In the powerful name of Jesus, amen.

PASTORS AND LEADERS

———— • ————

DEAR GOD, today is Sunday. For generations, it's been known as "the Lord's Day." As usual, I will attend a worship service at my church and be led by those you have called into the work of ministry. In 1 Timothy 3:1, the apostle Paul uses an appropriate word—*honorable*—to describe this calling: "This is a trustworthy saying: 'If someone aspires to be a church leader, he desires an *honorable* position.'" Sunday is the day of the week when I see our pastors and leaders, though I know they toil behind the scenes countless other hours as well. At times, our leaders must be exhausted from the ongoing demands of caring for your people. And church congregations can be fickle, sometimes holding higher expectations than any leader can live up to.

On this your day, Lord, please encourage, empower, and energize these special people. Please give them multiple blessings as they extend themselves to bless others. May you enrich their families and marriages, provide for their financial needs, and protect them from adversity. Please give them wisdom and guidance in ministering your Word. Please fill them with the power and might of your Holy Spirit, and use them to accomplish all you intend. For Jesus' sake, amen.

PRAYER THAT SEEMS UNANSWERED

———— • ————

KIND JESUS, WHO UNDERSTANDS SUFFERING, I know
I'm not the only person who has experienced the discouragement of seemingly unanswered prayers. What
I often forget is *your own* prayer that didn't go the way
you hoped or asked.

In the garden of Gethsemane, you were nearly crushed
by the anguish and stress you were enduring; you actually
sweated drops of blood. You were about to be betrayed
and crucified. Three times you pled with your Father to
take away your suffering; yet each time you said, "Not
my will, but yours."

Oh, sweet Jesus, *your* pain was horrible, much greater
than any pain of ours. Your pain wasn't just yours alone.
You took on the pain and sin of the whole world.

It's comforting to see that in your humanity, you
struggled. You can relate to my suffering. And just as you
drew strength from your relationship with God, I can do
the same.

Jesus, your unanswered prayer made it possible for
all of us to be forgiven and experience peace with God.
Our grateful hearts swell with thanks to you.

PRAYING BOLDLY

———— • ————

GRACIOUS GOD, you won my heart when I realized you loved me so much that you sent your Son to die for me. No other love in the world comes close to this kind of love. Over time, I saw you for who you are—a right and holy God, who provided a way for me, sinner that I am, to be reconciled to you through the gift of your Son. With a repentant heart, I come to you with reverence, affection, and faith.

I need your mercy, grace, and help each day, Lord, especially in those times when I'm not quick to see or admit how needy I am. You've urged me to draw near to you and to come boldly. May I not be timid or hesitant, but approach you with confidence, assured that you will provide for my needs.

I pray this from my heart.

So let us come boldly to the throne of our gracious God. There we will receive his mercy, and we will find grace to help us when we need it most.

HEBREWS 4:16

RAINY DAYS

— • —

GOD OF THE WEATHER, this morning I peered out my window to see gloomy showers. It's another gray day, and I am grumpy. How I long to gaze at a clear blue sky and experience the warmth of sunshine. Why another dreary day, Father?

And yet when I think about it, your Word describes rain much differently. The land where your Son, Jesus, ministered was a dry place, and people were often longing for the seasons that brought downpours—showers of blessing. The need for rain was a physical reality that demonstrated the desperate spiritual thirst inside everyone Jesus encountered—including us. Jesus, the biggest thirst-quencher of all time, stood and shouted to the crowds, "Anyone who is thirsty may come to me! Anyone who believes in me may come and drink! For the Scriptures declare, 'Rivers of living water will flow from his heart.'"

Lord, as I step over puddles today, help me to be grateful for your provision of water that I am presently enjoying—in abundance! Thank you that you are the Fountain of Life. Thank you that you are eager to quench my thirst. Amen.

SABBATH

———— • ————

Lᴏʀᴅ Gᴏᴅ, you set an example for us when you created all things in six days and rested from your work on the seventh. You instructed Moses and your people, "You have six days each week for your ordinary work, but the seventh day must be a Sabbath day of complete rest, a holy day dedicated to the Lᴏʀᴅ."

When Jesus walked the earth, he filled this command with rich, fresh meaning. He taught us that he himself was Lord of the Sabbath. Creator and Master, you made the Sabbath to be a day of rest, a blessing of restoration and refreshment for our souls.

Lord, too often I have thought of this day of rest as an obligation, something I had to practice in order to be truly good. I mistakenly thought that by obeying this command I could somehow earn more favor with you. How wrong I have been. You have given us a day that honors you while renewing and strengthening us. Thank you, God, for this needed gift. Help us to observe it wisely.

SMALL GROUPS

— • —

DEAR LORD, how thankful I am for the group of believers I meet with regularly. I have formed close bonds with these friends, and our weekly meetings nourish my soul. It's a place where we can share, encourage one another, and be transformed by your Word. We sense your presence in our midst, for you have promised to be with us whenever we gather in your name.

When you lived here on earth, you chose a small group—a group of twelve men you called your disciples. I can only imagine what it must have been like to have lived and traveled with you—to observe your matchless character, to witness your miracles, to feel your love. And yet, even living day in and day out with you, those men showed their true colors, not always understanding what you were teaching them. I am just like them.

The wonder of it all is that you are still very much with us—and in us, through your Spirit. You have asked us to represent you to one another in loving service. Lord Jesus, help me to be an accurate reflection of your grace, truth, and love to members of my group. Amen.

SPIRITUAL GROWTH

———— • ————

GOD WHO HELPS US GROW, I was touched when a friend delivered a flowering perennial to my doorstep one wintry day. You know I don't usually bring plants into my home because I am anything *but* a gardener. You've given some people the knack to make plants thrive, but I'm not one of them.

I'm trying to keep this plant alive until spring, God. It would be gratifying to plant it outside. I'll do my part by watering and pruning and snipping away dried leaves.

The growth I'm seeing in the plant—still alive!— reminds me of my own spiritual growth. Each morning when I read your Word, your truth nourishes and prunes my heart. It convinces me of your love and encourages me to ask for your help. It prompts me to confess thoughts and attitudes that are dragging me down. I sense that my relationship with you is being fed and is flourishing.

Thank you that spiritual growth is not reserved for just a few talented people. Thank you that it's available to us all. I'm grateful for your Word, Father. I don't know where I'd be without it.

SURGERY OF A CHILD

———— • ————

DEAR FATHER, the medical staff just rolled my son down the hospital corridor into a sterile surgical room, and I suddenly feel powerless and alone. Many "what if" scenarios pop into my mind. My fears begin to play scenes of what life would be like without my son. Please help me, God! In this moment, I realize again how much he means to me—his kind spirit, positive outlook, and creative ways. He brings so much joy to my life, and I can't imagine a day without him.

Please give the surgeon, the anesthesiologist, and the nursing staff alertness, precision, and full attention to their work. May you guide their hands, make them observant, and focus their considerable knowledge and experience through the course of this surgery. Help them to make good decisions. Please be by their side—helping them, and healing my son. For this I would be very grateful, and I ask it in Jesus' name, amen.

SURGERY OF A FRIEND

— • —

Caring Father, one of my friends is facing major surgery. Her situation will likely involve significant decisions, treatments, and routines in the weeks to come. I care deeply for my friend and will help however I can. I also appeal to you, God, for the kinds of help, strength, and healing only you can provide.

I remember a time when I had surgery and felt your presence with me, Lord. Just before I was wheeled into the operating room, a nurse turned to me and said, "I'll be praying for you. He's the Great Physician, you know." Those were such comforting words on which to float away . . .

Just as you encouraged me, please encourage my friend. Whether it's a person who sits at her bedside or a friend who chats with her on the phone, please prompt people around her to speak words that are brimming with kindness, encouragement, and understanding. Please send her exactly what she needs at just the right times—a book to read, an offer to run an errand, or a bowl of homemade soup to nourish her body and spirit.

Most of all, Father, please give my friend a sense of how much you love and care about her.

TAX SEASON

——— • ———

Dear Lord, preparing an annual tax return is always stressful for me. Each year I dread the forms, instructions, and new rules, fearful that I don't have the necessary documentation. The possibility that I might need to pay more taxes this year than I expected looms in the back of my mind.

I'm reminded, God, of your Son's clever reply when people tried to trick him into saying something against the government's tax collection. "Show me a Roman coin. Whose picture and title are stamped on it? . . . Give to Caesar what belongs to Caesar, and give to God what belongs to God."

As I approach tax season again, I'm reminded of my responsibility to pay taxes, and to do it truthfully and fairly. May I remember all the benefits I enjoy because of these monies: good highways, social services, a strong military, and much more. We are blessed by all of these things.

Help me understand each section of my tax forms and take advantage of the benefits to which I'm entitled. As I record my information accurately and completely, please guide me through each step. May I show respect for the authority under which you have placed me. Amen.

THANKS FOR
ABUNDANT LIFE

——— • ———

GENEROUS GOD, you offer us a rich and satisfying life. What an undeserved gift. The abundant life we inherit when we trust in Christ's sacrifice for our sins cost Jesus the ultimate price. And yet the monetary cost to us of becoming rich in Christ is . . . zero. You've explained to us in your Word that eternal life can't be bought with dollars, euros, pesos, or any other currency, nor can it be earned through church attendance, charitable gifts, or religious rules. It doesn't matter where we were born, where we live, where we work, or what we look like. No, the only way for us to receive your generous gift of eternal life is through faith in your Son, Jesus Christ.

Thank you that you not only forgive us and cleanse our hearts, but your Spirit pours out other gifts on us as well, such as kindness and patience. Because you conquered death, your Spirit gives us confidence that we, too, will inherit eternal life.

We're grateful for the overflowing benefits you've made available to us—each one freely given. What you want in return is our trust. Thank you, Father, for your endless riches.

THANKSGIVING DAY

——— • ———

LORD, when I pause to think about all that you have done in my life—the blessings you have lavished on my family, and the strength and protection you have given me—I am extremely grateful.

Too often, I'm prone to dwell on the challenges and problems I'm facing. I fret about things over which I have no control. My mind becomes troubled as I quickly forget how you've guided me in the past. I tend to focus on the wrong things.

Today, on this special day, I offer my sincere thanks for all you have done for me. More than that, I offer my gratitude and praise for who you are: Mighty God, Everlasting Father, Prince of Peace. You are worthy of my devotion, my honor, and my very life. Thank you, Father.

Thank you! Everything in me says "Thank you!"
    Angels listen as I sing my thanks.
I kneel in worship facing your holy temple
    and say it again: "Thank you!"
Thank you for your love,
    thank you for your faithfulness;
Most holy is your name,
    most holy is your Word.

PSALM 138:1-3, MSG

TRAVELING

— • —

ALL-SEEING GOD AND FATHER, I am setting out on a long journey. While I have planned carefully for this trip, I am apprehensive. The world is full of dangers and conflicts, and questions flood my mind. *What if my luggage is lost on one of the flights? What if I can't find my way in a strange city? What if there's a terrorist attack in the country I'm going to?* Please bring peace to my heart and let me rest in you, remembering your care for me in the past. May I relish opportunities to meet new people and experience parts of your wide world that I haven't seen before. Amen.

O LORD, . . .
You see me when I travel
    and when I rest at home.
    You know everything I do. . . .
You go before me and follow me.
    You place your hand of blessing on my head. . . .
I can never escape from your Spirit!
    I can never get away from your presence! . . .
If I ride the wings of the morning,
    if I dwell by the farthest oceans,
even there your hand will guide me,
    and your strength will support me.

PSALM 139:1, 3, 5, 7, 9-10

TRUSTING GOD DURING
DIFFICULT TIMES

—— • ——

FATHER GOD, some days, we go about our tasks and activities without thinking of you much at all, or seeking your wisdom, help, and perspective. If our lives are humming along without too many difficulties, we might have the illusion that we're holding things together pretty well. Until something goes terribly wrong—a loved one dies, a job ends, a chronic illness takes over, or a relationship is betrayed.

In times of pain and loss, Father, your Word offers tremendous guidance. We realize that although we don't know what's going to happen even later today, you know all our yesterdays, todays, and tomorrows. We can barely understand ourselves, but you see the whole human race and understand everything we do.

You remind us that success isn't having strength of our own. Rather, it comes from trusting you and relying on your unfailing love. Father, when troubles come our way, may we throw ourselves on you and draw upon your resources. You alone can provide us with the hope we need to keep going.

TRUSTING GOD WITH
OUR WORRIES

———— • ————

GOD, some mornings I say I want to trust you with all of my heart. But by midday it's not unusual for me to become aware that I'm worrying or complaining or trying to fix things that aren't mine to fix.

Help me to change my perspective. I want to be encouraged—even thankful—that your Spirit nudged me about what I was doing. Assist me in identifying my negative thoughts. Then I will look to you and ask for your help, which you are quick to provide.

Lord, I *do* want to trust you. Thank you for helping me see that my worrying, complaining, and controlling— my moments of unbelief—are not honoring to you. When I turn to you and tell you my needs, my worry starts to shrivel because of your peace.

Don't worry about anything; instead, pray about everything. Tell God what you need, and thank him for all he has done. Then you will experience God's peace, which exceeds anything we can understand. His peace will guard your hearts and minds as you live in Christ Jesus.

PHILIPPIANS 4:6-7

VALENTINE'S DAY

———— • ————

Loving Father, it's Valentine's Day, a special time for reaching out to people we love. Whatever way we choose to celebrate the day—with dinner, chocolate, flowers, cards—we're mindful that you are the Author, Architect, and Creator of love. More than that, you *are* love! We cannot begin to express what that means to us. The symbol of this day is a heart, and we offer you these words from our hearts each day.

Thank you for loving us first. You loved us before you were even a thought in our minds, before we realized who you are. You love us even when we are sinful and want to hide from you. It's no wonder your love is described as *unfailing*. Your love is the source of all human love, Father. Like a cinnamon plum tea bag that diffuses its flavor in hot water, may we share your incomparable love so those around us will taste it too.

We love each other because he loved us first.
1 JOHN 4:19

WHEN THERE'S
NOT ENOUGH

—— • ——

JESUS OF THE LOAVES AND FISH, many of us have lived through times when there wasn't enough . . . enough food, enough money, enough energy, enough employment. And some of us are living in that situation right now.

Over two thousand years ago, a multitude of people gathered on a hill to hear you speak. When you finished, you were concerned about their physical needs. "They have nothing left to eat. I don't want to send them away hungry." You cared about those people, God!

When your disciples asked you where they would find enough food for the immense crowd, your response was an example we can use in our "not enough" times.

You asked your disciples how much bread they had. You thanked your Father for it. You trusted him to multiply it. You asked your disciples to share it. And you urged them to remember the wonder of what they witnessed.

In our moments of not enough, Father, please help us assess what we have, thank you for it, trust you to multiply it, share it with others, and never forget the wonder of how you have provided for our needs. You surely are a loving and generous God.

WHEN THINGS GO WRONG

——— • ———

DEAR LORD, things haven't gone as I planned today, and I'm frustrated. I'm overwhelmed by all the things I need to do, ill-prepared for the many challenges coming my way.

Please settle my heart, calm my spirit, and remind me how you have directed me in the past. Give me proper perspective, and cut my problems down to their real size. Have these details escaped your notice? Have you been busy helping someone else and forgotten me? Of course not!

You are the sovereign God who made heaven and earth. You breathed your very life into your children. You chose your special people and instructed them in your ways. And you sent your one and only Son to be our Redeemer and Savior.

I hand you my problems and concerns, Father. Your arm is strong to save, and I can trust you to accomplish what is good and glorifies you. Thank you for your faithfulness to me and to all generations. Amen.

WHEN WE DON'T KNOW
WHAT TO DO

———— • ————

POWERFUL GOD, sometimes we find ourselves in bleak situations, and we just don't know what to do. In the Old Testament, when King Jehoshaphat heard that a vast army was marching against him, he was terrified. Immediately, he turned to you. He knew you were the powerful God of his ancestors. You alone are God in heaven, and you are ruler of all the kingdoms of the earth. No one can stand against you.

After reviewing some of the things you'd done in the past, this trusting king talked to you about the imminent crisis facing him. I love the way he ended his prayer, Father. "We are powerless against this mighty army that is about to attack us. We do not know what to do, but we are looking to you for help."

Mighty Father, for times when we find ourselves in the middle of our own desperate situations, Jehoshaphat's prayer can be our prayer. *We do not know what to do, but we are looking to you for help.*

Thank you that you heard and rescued Jehoshaphat. Thank you that you hear us and come to our aid today.

WINTER MORNING

—— • ——

CREATOR OF ALL SEASONS, I awoke this morning to a dismal winter's day. The beauty and magic of Christmas have passed, and there is still so much more winter to endure. The cold and darkness of these days weigh me down like a wet blanket.

Father, you have set the sun, moon, and earth in their places. You have determined the seasons, showing us the cycles of life, death, and resurrection. You have made all things for your glory and for us to enjoy, and you have called them "very good."

When the winter rains come, God, may I reflect that rain is a blessing, nourishing the earth. When it is overcast, may I remember your presence in the clouds of Mount Sinai where you gave Moses your commandments for your people. And when it snows, may I recall the prophet's words: "Though your sins are like scarlet, I will make them as white as snow." These weather conditions are signs that proclaim your constant care, not only for your good earth, but for your people—for me—upon whom you have lavished your love. Thank you. Amen.

WISDOM

—— • ——

LOVING FATHER, not only do you possess wisdom; you *are* Wisdom. Not a day goes by without my needing and wanting your direction. Sometimes I speak too quickly or my attitude is selfish. Or I attempt to solve someone else's problems.

When I realize what I'm doing, God, a gracious first step toward change, may I stop and seek your insight. My failures are opportunities to ask you for your help— again. Thank you that you are always available and that no problem is too difficult for you. Because you see my past, my present, and my future, your viewpoint is all-encompassing. I'm grateful that your supply of wisdom is endless and your solutions are abundant.

You tell us that all wisdom's ways are satisfying and that we're happiest when we hold on to wisdom tightly. I cling to you, Father, thanking you for offering me knowledge with great joy!

> If you need wisdom, ask our generous God, and he will give it to you. He will not rebuke you for asking.
> JAMES 1:5

WORK

—— • ——

ᶠFATHER, I am inspired to do my job well because of the example of Bezalel.

The Old Testament records that Bezalel was a master craftsman who worked on the construction and furnishings of the Tabernacle, the place where you would dwell amongst your people, and he used with excellence the gifts you gave him. In addition to his special abilities, you also filled him with your Spirit and gave him great wisdom. All through history, Father, you have gifted people with a variety of abilities, and you often called them to do amazing work to fulfill your purposes.

Gracious God, we want to use the gifts you've given us to the best of our abilities. As we follow the paths where you lead us, please stir our minds, move our spirits, and quicken our hearts so that we will always work to please you.

Work with enthusiasm, as though you were working for the Lord rather than for people.
EPHESIANS 6:7

WORLD LEADERS

——— • ———

SOVEREIGN LORD, you are God over all the nations of
the whole world . . . and yet you are personally engaged
with each one of us. This brings us comfort and hope—
not just for our personal circle of family, job, friends, and
activities, but also for world events. When we hear about
developments in countries we're not familiar with, we're
grateful you wield supreme power there, too. You hold the
whole world in your hands as lovingly as you hold each of
our individual lives.

This prompts us to pray for world leaders around the
globe. You created each of them, Father, and you alone
know their hearts and minds. History records heads of
government who followed you and were instrumental in
bringing your righteousness and justice to various situations. History also records leaders who didn't know you,
yet whose hearts were directed by you nonetheless.

Please help each of these select few to make wise
choices that ultimately honor you and honor the people
they serve. And even if they don't make choices that seem
wise, we acknowledge that you remain the supreme Ruler
of the world. Thank you, Father, that you are always in
control.

Prayer is our declaration of dependence upon the Lord.

PHILIP YANCEY

PART TWO

Prayers from
the Bible

PRAISE FOR
ANSWERED PRAYER

My heart rejoices in the LORD!
    The LORD has made me strong.
Now I have an answer for my enemies;
    I rejoice because you rescued me.
No one is holy like the LORD!
    There is no one besides you;
    there is no Rock like our God.

Lord, I remember a time in my life when I desperately needed hope. I found it while reading the story of Hannah, the mother of Samuel, the greatest Old Testament judge in Israel. Hannah was straight-up honest with you about her bitterness and anguish, and yet her response is a beautiful example for me. She poured out the troubles of her heart to you. Hannah learned that you are a God who listens, cares, and can be trusted. I needed to know that in my life, Father. Thank you, God, for using Hannah's story to impress me to trust you in my story.

GOD'S HELP IN TIMES
OF TROUBLE

PSALM 20:1-5

In times of trouble, may the LORD answer your cry.
    May the name of the God of Jacob keep you safe
        from all harm.
May he send you help from his sanctuary
    and strengthen you from Jerusalem.
May he remember all your gifts
    and look favorably on your burnt offerings.

May he grant your heart's desires
    and make all your plans succeed.
May we shout for joy when we hear of your victory
    and raise a victory banner in the name of
        our God.
May the LORD answer all your prayers.

*Father, as I've cried out to you in times of trouble, you have
helped me and strengthened me. Over the years, you've not
only granted me my heart's desires—you've thrown in extra
blessings I wouldn't have even thought to ask for. What a
gracious God you are! Amen.*

PSALM OF THE SHEPHERD

PSALM 23

The LORD is my shepherd;
    I have all that I need.
He lets me rest in green meadows;
    he leads me beside peaceful streams.
    He renews my strength.
He guides me along right paths,
    bringing honor to his name.
Even when I walk
    through the darkest valley,
I will not be afraid,
    for you are close beside me.
Your rod and your staff
    protect and comfort me.
You prepare a feast for me
    in the presence of my enemies.
You honor me by anointing my head with oil.
    My cup overflows with blessings.
Surely your goodness and unfailing love will
        pursue me
    all the days of my life,
and I will live in the house of the LORD
    forever.

Kind Father, as a shepherd holds a little lamb, please wrap your loving arms around me and carry me. Oh, how I need your love. Help me not to be afraid, because you are with me—not just in the uncertainties of life, but even in death. You are the only one who will walk with me there, Father. Thank you that your goodness and unfailing love will continue to chase me for the rest of my days on earth—and forever!

SEEKING GOD WHILE
WE WAIT

PSALM 27:7-14

Hear me as I pray, O LORD.
    Be merciful and answer me!
My heart has heard you say, "Come and talk
        with me."
    And my heart responds, "LORD, I am coming."
Do not turn your back on me.
    Do not reject your servant in anger.
    You have always been my helper.
Don't leave me now; don't abandon me,
    O God of my salvation!
Even if my father and mother abandon me,
    the LORD will hold me close.

Teach me how to live, O LORD.
    Lead me along the right path,
    for my enemies are waiting for me.
Do not let me fall into their hands.
    For they accuse me of things I've never done;
    with every breath they threaten me with violence.
Yet I am confident I will see the LORD's goodness
    while I am here in the land of the living.

Wait patiently for the LORD.
　　Be brave and courageous.
　　Yes, wait patiently for the LORD.

Lord, times of waiting have often become incredible learn-ing and growing lessons for me. You've helped me see that you understand my needs much better than I do. Thank you, Father, that you have used seeming delays to fortify my faith in you.

———— ❖ ❖ ————

We must lay before
Him what is in us, not
what ought to be in us.

C. S. LEWIS

GOD HEARS OUR CRY

PSALM 28:1-2, 6-7

I pray to you, O LORD, my rock.
    Do not turn a deaf ear to me.
For if you are silent,
    I might as well give up and die.
Listen to my prayer for mercy
    as I cry out to you for help,
    as I lift my hands toward your holy sanctuary. . . .

Praise the LORD!
    For he has heard my cry for mercy.
The LORD is my strength and shield.
    I trust him with all my heart.
He helps me, and my heart is filled with joy.
    I burst out in songs of thanksgiving.

Holy God, you are my Rock, whom I trust. With your strength, I am more equipped to face my challenges. Thank you for the protection you provide.

PRIORITIES

LORD, remind me how brief my time on earth will be.
Remind me that my days are numbered—
how fleeting my life is.
You have made my life no longer than the width of
my hand.
My entire lifetime is just a moment to you;
at best, each of us is but a breath.

We are merely moving shadows,
and all our busy rushing ends in nothing.
We heap up wealth,
not knowing who will spend it.
And so, Lord, where do I put my hope?
My only hope is in you.

*God, you live in eternity, and it's hard for us to get our minds
around that. In comparison to you, our lives seem like meteors
that pass quickly through the sky. Even if we saved millions
of dollars during our short lifetime, we couldn't take a penny
of it with us when we die. What we can take with us is our
relationship with you. Though we shouldn't put our hope in
time or money, we're safe to put our hope in you, God. Thank
you that you are the same yesterday, today, and forever.*

Oh! It is a glorious
fact, that prayers are
noticed in heaven.

C. H. SPURGEON

PRAYER FOR DELIVERANCE

PSALM 40

I waited patiently for the LORD to help me,
    and he turned to me and heard my cry.
He lifted me out of the pit of despair,
    out of the mud and the mire.
He set my feet on solid ground
    and steadied me as I walked along.
He has given me a new song to sing,
    a hymn of praise to our God.
Many will see what he has done and be amazed.
    They will put their trust in the LORD.

Oh, the joys of those who trust the LORD,
    who have no confidence in the proud
    or in those who worship idols.
O LORD my God, you have performed many
      wonders for us.
    Your plans for us are too numerous to list.
    You have no equal.
If I tried to recite all your wonderful deeds,
    I would never come to the end of them.

You take no delight in sacrifices or offerings.
> Now that you have made me listen, I finally
> > understand—
> you don't require burnt offerings or sin offerings.
Then I said, "Look, I have come.
> As is written about me in the Scriptures:
I take joy in doing your will, my God,
> for your instructions are written on my heart."

I have told all your people about your justice.
> I have not been afraid to speak out,
> > as you, O Lord, well know.
I have not kept the good news of your justice hidden
> > in my heart;
> I have talked about your faithfulness and saving
> > power.
I have told everyone in the great assembly
> of your unfailing love and faithfulness.

Lord, don't hold back your tender mercies from me.
> Let your unfailing love and faithfulness always
> > protect me.
For troubles surround me—
> too many to count!
My sins pile up so high
> I can't see my way out.
They outnumber the hairs on my head.
> I have lost all courage.

Please, LORD, rescue me!
    Come quickly, LORD, and help me.
May those who try to destroy me
    be humiliated and put to shame.
May those who take delight in my trouble
    be turned back in disgrace.
Let them be horrified by their shame,
    for they said, "Aha! We've got him now!"

But may all who search for you
    be filled with joy and gladness in you.
May those who love your salvation
    repeatedly shout, "The LORD is great!"
As for me, since I am poor and needy,
    let the Lord keep me in his thoughts.
You are my helper and my savior.
    O my God, do not delay.

*Lord God, you have shown me your mercy and grace
in countless ways. I join the chorus and say, "The LORD
is great!"*

PRAYER FOR THE DISCOURAGED

PSALM 42:5-6, 8

Why am I discouraged?
  Why is my heart so sad?
I will put my hope in God!
  I will praise him again—
  my Savior and my God! . . .

Each day the LORD pours his unfailing love upon me,
  and through each night I sing his songs,
  praying to God who gives me life.

Wonderful Counselor, when I think back to the low points in my life, I'm thankful that your Word encouraged me and helped hoist me out of slippery pits. One time in particular, I felt prompted by you to get away for a day with my Bible and meditate. If I hadn't sought help from you, I shudder to think of how different my life might be today. Thank you, God, for directing me to turn to you.

DO IT AGAIN, LORD

PSALM 44:1-8

O God, we have heard it with our own ears—
    our ancestors have told us
of all you did in their day,
    in days long ago:
You drove out the pagan nations by your power
    and gave all the land to our ancestors.
You crushed their enemies
    and set our ancestors free.
They did not conquer the land with their swords;
    it was not their own strong arm that gave them
        victory.
It was your right hand and strong arm
    and the blinding light from your face that helped
        them,
    for you loved them.

You are my King and my God.
    You command victories for Israel.
Only by your power can we push back our enemies;
    only in your name can we trample our foes.
I do not trust in my bow;
    I do not count on my sword to save me.

You are the one who gives us victory over our
   enemies;
  you disgrace those who hate us.
O God, we give glory to you all day long
  and constantly praise your name.

*Our King and our God, whatever kinds of enemies we are
facing today, may we remember your deliverances in the past.
As we reflect on your faithfulness, help us to realize you will
never leave us or forsake us. Thank you that your presence is
always with us.*

❖ ❖

> **In prayer it is better to have
> a heart without words
> than words without a heart.**
>
> JOHN BUNYAN

A PRAYER OF REPENTANCE

PSALM 51:1-17

Have mercy on me, O God,
    because of your unfailing love.
Because of your great compassion,
    blot out the stain of my sins.
Wash me clean from my guilt.
    Purify me from my sin.
For I recognize my rebellion;
    it haunts me day and night.
Against you, and you alone, have I sinned;
    I have done what is evil in your sight.
You will be proved right in what you say,
    and your judgment against me is just.
For I was born a sinner—
    yes, from the moment my mother conceived me.
But you desire honesty from the womb,
    teaching me wisdom even there.

Purify me from my sins, and I will be clean;
    wash me, and I will be whiter than snow.
Oh, give me back my joy again;
    you have broken me—
        now let me rejoice.

Don't keep looking at my sins.
> Remove the stain of my guilt.

Create in me a clean heart, O God.
> Renew a loyal spirit within me.

Do not banish me from your presence,
> and don't take your Holy Spirit from me.

Restore to me the joy of your salvation,
> and make me willing to obey you.

Then I will teach your ways to rebels,
> and they will return to you.

Forgive me for shedding blood, O God who saves;
> then I will joyfully sing of your forgiveness.

Unseal my lips, O Lord,
> that my mouth may praise you.

You do not desire a sacrifice, or I would offer one.
> You do not want a burnt offering.

The sacrifice you desire is a broken spirit.
> You will not reject a broken and repentant heart,
> > O God.

Forgiving Father, help me to be quick to confess my sins to you and praise you for your loving response.

OVERWHELMED

PSALM 61:1-3

O God, listen to my cry!
  Hear my prayer!
From the ends of the earth,
  I cry to you for help
  when my heart is overwhelmed.
Lead me to the towering rock of safety,
  for you are my safe refuge,
  a fortress where my enemies cannot reach me.

God of the universe, no matter where we go or how overwhelmed we feel, we're grateful that you see us, listen to us, and help us. May we cling tightly to you and trust you to lead us out of our difficulties and into a better place. Thank you for being our safe refuge, Father.

THE LORD'S PRAYER

Our Father in heaven,
>   may your name be kept holy.
May your Kingdom come soon.
May your will be done on earth,
>   as it is in heaven.
Give us today the food we need,
and forgive us our sins,
>   as we have forgiven those who sin against us.
And don't let us yield to temptation,
>   but rescue us from the evil one.

Kind Jesus, thank you for showing us how to pray to our loving Father. May we continually praise you and pray for your work around the world. Help us trust you to provide all that we need. We are grateful for your forgiveness; compel us to extend forgiveness to others. In our daily challenges, please empower us to resist evil. Amen.

FAITH FOR THE IMPOSSIBLE

"Roll the stone aside," Jesus told them.

But Martha, the dead man's sister, protested, "Lord, he has been dead for four days. The smell will be terrible."

Jesus responded, "Didn't I tell you that you would see God's glory if you believe?" So they rolled the stone aside. Then Jesus looked up to heaven and said, "Father, thank you for hearing me. You always hear me, but I said it out loud for the sake of all these people standing here, so that they will believe you sent me." Then Jesus shouted, "Lazarus, come out!" And the dead man came out, his hands and feet bound in graveclothes, his face wrapped in a headcloth. Jesus told them, "Unwrap him and let him go!"

Many of the people who were with Mary believed in Jesus when they saw this happen.

Father, the words of your Son's prayer encourage us that you hear our prayers too. May we pray to you often—for our own needs and the needs of others.

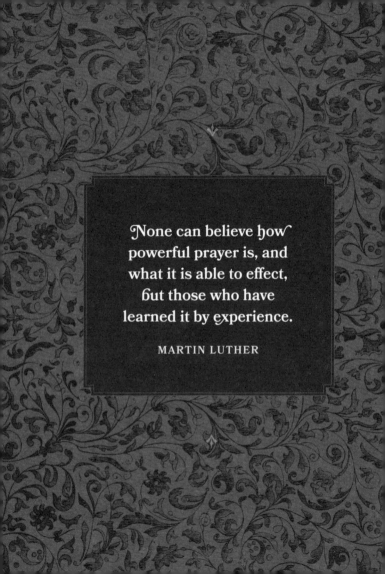

None can believe how powerful prayer is, and what it is able to effect, but those who have learned it by experience.

MARTIN LUTHER

ᛁNNER STRENGTH THROUGH GOD'S SPIRIT

EPHESIANS 3:14-20

I fall to my knees and pray to the Father, the Creator of everything in heaven and on earth. I pray that from his glorious, unlimited resources he will empower you with inner strength through his Spirit. Then Christ will make his home in your hearts as you trust in him. Your roots will grow down into God's love and keep you strong. And may you have the power to understand, as all God's people should, how wide, how long, how high, and how deep his love is. May you experience the love of Christ, though it is too great to understand fully. Then you will be made complete with all the fullness of life and power that comes from God.

Now all glory to God, who is able, through his mighty power at work within us, to accomplish infinitely more than we might ask or think.

Thank you, Father, for your unfailing love. Though it is so vast that it can't be measured, I can experience it daily in my heart. Please fill me with your mighty power, and accomplish in me and through me more than I could ever imagine.

PRAYERS FROM THE BIBLE

PRAYER FOR CHRISTIAN WORKERS

PHILIPPIANS 1:3-11

Every time I think of you, I give thanks to my God. Whenever I pray, I make my requests for all of you with joy, for you have been my partners in spreading the Good News about Christ from the time you first heard it until now. And I am certain that God, who began the good work within you, will continue his work until it is finally finished on the day when Christ Jesus returns.

So it is right that I should feel as I do about all of you, for you have a special place in my heart. You share with me the special favor of God . . . in defending and confirming the truth of the Good News. God knows how much I love you and long for you with the tender compassion of Christ Jesus.

I pray that your love will overflow more and more, and that you will keep on growing in knowledge and understanding. For I want you to understand what really matters, so that you may live pure and blameless lives until the day of Christ's return. May you always be filled with the fruit of your salvation—the righteous character

produced in your life by Jesus Christ—for this
will bring much glory and praise to God.

*Father, I have been privileged to be a partner in spreading
your Good News to others, seeing the "fruit of your salvation"
in the lives of your children throughout the world. I humbly
offer this prayer for myself and also for them.*

Nothing is too great and
nothing is too small to commit
into the hands of the Lord.

A. W. PINK

A PRAYER OF EMPOWERMENT

COLOSSIANS 1:9-14

We have not stopped praying for you since we first heard about you. We ask God to give you complete knowledge of his will and to give you spiritual wisdom and understanding. Then the way you live will always honor and please the Lord, and your lives will produce every kind of good fruit. All the while, you will grow as you learn to know God better and better.

We also pray that you will be strengthened with all his glorious power so you will have all the endurance and patience you need. May you be filled with joy, always thanking the Father. He has enabled you to share in the inheritance that belongs to his people, who live in the light. For he has rescued us from the kingdom of darkness and transferred us into the Kingdom of his dear Son, who purchased our freedom and forgave our sins.

Father, we offer this prayer for fellow believers, and in addition, we take encouragement for ourselves. Give us knowledge of your will and empower us to live it out! In the strong name of Jesus, amen.

A BLESSING

Now may the God of peace—
  who brought up from the dead our Lord Jesus,
the great Shepherd of the sheep,
  and ratified an eternal covenant with his blood—
may he equip you with all you need
  for doing his will.
May he produce in you,
  through the power of Jesus Christ,
every good thing that is pleasing to him.
  All glory to him forever and ever! Amen.

Father, please bring wholeness and blessing to each person reading or hearing this prayer. Convince us that because of Jesus' death and resurrection, we can trust you to grow us into people who will please you and be productive for you. In the victorious name of Jesus, amen.

Thou art coming to a King,
Large petitions with thee bring;
For his grace and power are such,
None can ever ask too much.

JOHN NEWTON

PART THREE

Prayers from Hymns

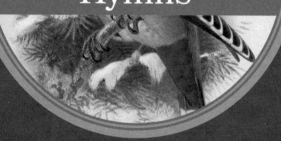

ABIDE WITH ME

HENRY F. LYTE, 1847

Abide with me: fast falls the eventide;
The darkness deepens; Lord, with me abide!
When other helpers fail, and comforts flee,
Help of the helpless, O abide with me.

Swift to its close ebbs out life's little day;
Earth's joys grow dim, its glories pass away;
Change and decay in all around I see.
O Thou who changest not, abide with me.

I need Thy presence every passing hour;
What but Thy grace can foil the tempter's power?
Who, like Thyself, my guide and stay can be?
Through cloud and sunshine, Lord, abide with me.

I fear no foe, with Thee at hand to bless;
Ills have no weight, and tears no bitterness.
Where is death's sting? Where, grave, thy victory?
I triumph still, if Thou abide with me.

Hold Thou Thy cross before my closing eyes;
Shine through the gloom and point me to the skies:
Heav'n's morning breaks, and earth's vain shadows flee;
In life, in death, O Lord, abide with me.

ANOTHER YEAR IS DAWNING

FRANCES R. HAVERGAL, 1874

Another year is dawning! Dear Father, let it be,
In working or in waiting, another year with Thee;
Another year of progress, another year of praise,
Another year of proving Thy presence all the days.

Another year of mercies, of faithfulness and grace,
Another year of gladness, in the shining of Thy face;
Another year of leaning upon Thy loving breast,
Another year of trusting, of quiet, happy rest.

Another year of service, of witness for Thy love,
Another year of training for holier work above;
Another year is dawning! Dear Father, let it be,
On earth, or else in heaven, another year for Thee.

AS WITH GLADNESS MEN OF OLD

WILLIAM C. DIX, 1860

As with gladness men of old
Did the guiding star behold;
As with joy they hailed its light,
Leading onward, beaming bright,
So, most gracious Lord, may we
Evermore be led to Thee.

As with joyful steps they sped
To that lowly manger bed,
There to bend the knee before
Him Whom heav'n and earth adore,
So may we with willing feet
Ever seek the mercy seat.

As they offered gifts most rare
At that manger rude and bare,
So may we with holy joy,
Pure and free from sin's alloy,
All our costliest treasures bring,
Christ, to Thee our heav'nly King.

COME, THOU LONG EXPECTED JESUS

CHARLES WESLEY, 1744

Come, Thou long expected Jesus,
Born to set Thy people free;
From our fears and sins release us;
Let us find our rest in Thee.
Israel's strength and consolation,
Hope of all the earth Thou art;
Dear desire of every nation,
Joy of every longing heart.

Born Thy people to deliver,
Born a child and yet a king.
Born to reign in us forever,
Now Thy gracious kingdom bring.
By thine own eternal Spirit
Rule in all our hearts alone;
By Thine all sufficient merit,
Raise us to Thy glorious throne.

COME, YE DISCONSOLATE

STANZAS 1–2, THOMAS MOORE, 1824
STANZA 3, THOMAS HASTINGS, 1831

Come, ye disconsolate, where'er ye languish;
Come to the mercy seat, fervently kneel;
Here bring your wounded hearts, here tell your anguish;
Earth has no sorrow that heav'n cannot heal.

Joy of the desolate, Light of the straying,
Hope of the penitent, fadeless and pure,
Here speaks the Comforter, tenderly saying,
"Earth has no sorrow that heav'n cannot cure."

Here see the Bread of Life; see waters flowing
Forth from the throne of God, pure from above;
Come to the feast of love; come, ever knowing
Earth has no sorrow but heav'n can remove.

DEAR LORD AND FATHER OF MANKIND

JOHN G. WHITTIER, 1872

Dear Lord and Father of mankind,
Forgive our foolish ways!
Reclothe us in our rightful mind;
In purer lives Thy service find,
In deeper rev'rence, praise.

In simple trust like theirs who heard,
Beside the Syrian Sea,
The gracious calling of the Lord,
Let us, like them, without a word,
Rise up and follow Thee.

Drop Thy still dews of quietness,
Till all our strivings cease;
Take from our souls the strain and stress,
And let our ordered lives confess
The beauty of Thy peace.

Breathe through the heats of our desire
Thy coolness and Thy balm;
Let sense be dumb, let flesh retire;
Speak through the earthquake, wind, and fire,
O still small voice of calm!

FAIREST LORD JESUS

MÜNSTER GESANGBUCH, 1677
Stanzas 1–3 translator unknown, 1850
Stanza 4 translated by Joseph A. Seiss, 1873

Fairest Lord Jesus!
Ruler of all nature,
O Thou of God
And man the Son!
Thee will I cherish,
Thee will I honor,
Thou, my soul's glory, joy, and crown!

Fair are the meadows,
Fairer still the woodlands,
Robed in the blooming garb of spring:
Jesus is fairer,
Jesus is purer,
Who makes the woeful heart to sing.

Fair is the sunshine,
Fairer still the moonlight,
And all the twinkling starry host:
Jesus shines brighter,
Jesus shines purer,
Than all the angels heav'n can boast.

Beautiful Savior!
Lord of the nations!
Son of God and Son of Man!
Glory and honor,
Praise, adoration,
Now and forevermore be Thine!

———— ❖ ❖ ————

137

GREAT IS THY FAITHFULNESS

THOMAS O. CHISHOLM, 1923

Great is Thy faithfulness, O God my Father,
There is no shadow of turning with Thee;
Thou changest not, Thy compassions they fail not;
As Thou hast been Thou forever wilt be.

(Refrain)
Great is Thy faithfulness!
Great is Thy faithfulness!
Morning by morning new mercies I see;
All I have needed Thy hand hath provided.
Great is Thy faithfulness, Lord, unto me!

Summer and winter, and springtime and harvest,
Sun, moon, and stars in their courses above
Join with all nature in manifold witness
To Thy great faithfulness, mercy, and love.

Pardon for sin and a peace that endureth,
Thy own dear presence to cheer and to guide;
Strength for today and bright hope for tomorrow,
Blessings all mine, with ten thousand beside!*

Holy, Holy, Holy!

REGINALD HEBER, 1826

Holy, holy, holy! Lord God Almighty!
Early in the morning our song shall rise to Thee;
Holy, holy, holy! Merciful and mighty!
God in three persons, blessed Trinity!

Holy, holy, holy! All the saints adore Thee,
Casting down their golden crowns around the glassy sea;
Cherubim and seraphim falling down before Thee,
Which wert and art, and evermore shalt be.

Holy, holy, holy! Though the darkness hide Thee,
Though the eye of sinful man Thy glory may not see,
Only Thou art holy; there is none beside Thee,
Perfect in pow'r, in love, and purity.

Holy, holy, holy! Lord God Almighty!
All Thy works shall praise Thy name, in earth, and sky,
and sea;
Holy, holy, holy! Merciful and mighty!
God in three persons, blessed Trinity!

HOLY SPIRIT, LIGHT DIVINE

ANDREW REED, 1817

Holy Spirit, Light divine,
Shine upon this heart of mine;
Chase the shades of night away,
Turn my darkness into day.

Holy Spirit, Power divine,
Cleanse this guilty heart of mine;
Long hath sin without control
Held dominion o'er my soul.

Holy Spirit, Joy divine,
Cheer this saddened heart of mine;
Bid my many woes depart,
Heal my wounded, bleeding heart.

Holy Spirit, all divine,
Dwell within this heart of mine;
Cast down every idol throne,
Reign supreme, and reign alone.

I NEED THEE EVERY HOUR

ANNIE S. HAWKS, 1872

I need Thee every hour,
Most gracious Lord;
No tender voice like Thine
Can peace afford.

(Refrain)
I need Thee, O I need Thee;
Every hour I need Thee;
O bless me now, my Savior,
I come to Thee!

I need Thee every hour,
Stay Thou near by;
Temptations lose their pow'r
When Thou art nigh.

I need Thee every hour
In joy or pain;
Come quickly and abide
Or life is vain.

I need Thee every hour,
Most Holy One;
O make me Thine indeed,
Thou blessed Son!

JESUS, I AM
RESTING, RESTING

JEAN S. PIGOTT, 1876

Jesus, I am resting, resting
In the joy of what Thou art;
I am finding out the greatness
Of Thy loving heart.
Thou hast bid me gaze upon Thee,
And Thy beauty fills my soul,
For by Thy transforming power,
Thou hast made me whole.

(Refrain)
Jesus, I am resting, resting
In the joy of what Thou art;
I am finding out the greatness
Of Thy loving heart.

O, how great Thy loving kindness,
Vaster, broader than the sea!
O, how marvelous Thy goodness,
Lavished all on me!
Yes, I rest in Thee, Beloved,
Know what wealth of grace is Thine,
Know Thy certainty of promise,
And have made it mine.

Simply trusting Thee, Lord Jesus,
I behold Thee as Thou art,
And Thy love, so pure, so changeless,
Satisfies my heart;
Satisfies its deepest longings,
Meets, supplies its every need,
Compasseth me round with blessings:
Thine is love indeed!

Ever lift Thy face upon me
As I work and wait for Thee;
Resting 'neath Thy smile, Lord Jesus,
Earth's dark shadows flee.
Brightness of my Father's glory,
Sunshine of my Father's face,
Keep me ever trusting, resting,
Fill me with Thy grace.

JESUS, LOVER OF MY SOUL

CHARLES WESLEY, 1740

Jesus, Lover of my soul,
Let me to Thy bosom fly,
While the nearer waters roll,
While the tempest still is high:
Hide me, O my Savior, hide,
Till the storm of life is past;
Safe into the haven guide;
O receive my soul at last!

Other refuge have I none;
Hangs my helpless soul on Thee;
Leave, ah! leave me not alone,
Still support and comfort me.
All my trust on Thee is stayed,
All my help from Thee I bring;
Cover my defenseless head
With the shadow of Thy wing.

Thou, O Christ, art all I want;
More than all in Thee I find;
Raise the fallen, cheer the faint,
Heal the sick, and lead the blind.

Just and holy is Thy name,
I am all unrighteousness;
False and full of sin I am,
Thou art full of truth and grace.

Plenteous grace with Thee is found,
Grace to cover all my sin;
Let the healing streams abound;
Make and keep me pure within.
Thou of life the fountain art,
Freely let me take of Thee;
Spring Thou up within my heart,
Rise to all eternity.

JESUS, THE VERY THOUGHT OF THEE

ATTRIBUTED TO BERNARD OF CLAIRVAUX, CA. 1150
Translated by Edward Caswall, 1849

Jesus, the very thought of Thee
With sweetness fills my breast;
But sweeter far Thy face to see,
And in Thy presence rest.

Nor voice can sing, nor heart can frame,
Nor can the memory find
A sweeter sound than Thy blest name,
O Savior of mankind!

O Hope of every contrite heart,
O Joy of all the meek,
To those who fall, how kind Thou art!
How good to those who seek!

But what to those who find? Ah! this
Nor tongue nor pen can show,
The love of Jesus, what it is
None but His loved ones know.

JESUS, THOU JOY OF LOVING HEARTS

ATTRIBUTED TO BERNARD OF CLAIRVAUX, CA. 1150
Translated by Ray Palmer, 1858

Jesus, thou Joy of loving hearts,
Thou fount of life, Thou Light of men,
From the best bless that earth imparts,
We turn unfilled to Thee again.

Thy truth unchanged hath ever stood;
Thou savest those that on Thee call;
To them that seek Thee, Thou art good,
To them that find Thee, all in all.

We taste Thee, O Thou living Bread,
And long to feast upon Thee still;
We drink of Thee, the Fountainhead,
And thirst our souls from Thee to fill.

Our restless spirits yearn for Thee,
Where'er our changeful lot is cast;
Glad, when Thy gracious smile we see,
Blest, when our faith can hold Thee fast.

O Jesus, ever with us stay,
Make all our moments calm and bright;
Chase the dark night of sin away,
Shed o'er the world Thy holy light.

JOYFUL, JOYFUL,
WE ADORE THEE

HENRY VAN DYKE, 1907

Joyful, joyful, we adore Thee,
God of glory, Lord of love;
Hearts unfold like flow'rs before Thee,
Opening to the sun above.
Melt the clouds of sin and sadness;
Drive the dark of doubt away;
Giver of immortal gladness,
Fill us with the light of day!

All Thy works with joy surround Thee,
Earth and heav'n reflect Thy rays,
Stars and angels sing around Thee,
Center of unbroken praise.
Field and forest, vale and mountain,
Flowery meadow, flashing sea,
Chanting bird and flowing fountain
Call us to rejoice in Thee.

Thou art giving and forgiving
Ever blessing, ever blest,
Wellspring of the joy of living,
Ocean depth of happy rest!

Thou our Father, Christ our Brother—
    All who live in love are Thine;
Teach us how to love each other,
    Lift us to the joy divine.

Mortals join the mighty chorus
Which the morning stars began;
Father love is reigning o'er us,
Brother love binds man to man.
Ever singing, march we onward,
    Victors in the midst of strife;
Joyful music leads us sunward
    In the triumph song of life.

———— ✦ ✦ ————

Praying unlocks
the doors of heaven
and releases the
power of God.

BILLY GRAHAM

JUST A CLOSER WALK WITH THEE

SOURCE UNKNOWN

I am weak, but Thou art strong;
Jesus, keep me from all wrong;
I'll be satisfied as long
As I walk, let me walk close to Thee.

(Refrain)
Just a closer walk with Thee,
Grant it, Jesus, is my plea,
Daily walking close to Thee,
Let it be, dear Lord, let it be.

Thro' this world of toil and snares,
If I falter, Lord, who cares?
Who with me my burden shares?
None but Thee, dear Lord, none but Thee.

When my feeble life is o'er,
Time for me will be no more;
Guide me gently, safely o'er
To Thy kingdom shore, to Thy shore.

PRAYERS FROM HYMNS

JUST AS I AM, WITHOUT ONE PLEA

CHARLOTTE ELLIOTT, 1834

Just as I am, without one plea
But that Thy blood was shed for me,
And that Thou bidd'st me come to Thee,
O Lamb of God, I come! I come!

Just as I am, and waiting not
To rid my soul of one dark blot,
To Thee whose blood can cleanse each spot,
O Lamb of God, I come! I come!

Just as I am, though tossed about
With many a conflict, many a doubt,
Fightings and fears within, without,
O Lamb of God, I come! I come!

Just as I am, poor, wretched, blind;
Sight, riches, healing of the mind,
Yea, all I need, in Thee I find,
O Lamb of God, I come! I come!

Just as I am, Thou wilt receive,
Wilt welcome, pardon, cleanse, relieve;
Because Thy promise I believe,
O Lamb of God, I come! I come!

KING OF THE AGES

KEITH GETTY AND STUART TOWNEND, 2002

King of the Ages, Almighty God;
Perfect love, ever just and true.
Who will not fear You and bring You praise?
All the nations will come to You.

Your ways of love have won my heart,
And brought me joy unending;
Your saving power at work in me,
Bringing peace and the hope of glory.

Your arms of love are reaching out
To every soul that seeks You.
Your light will shine in all the earth
Bringing grace and a great salvation.

The day will come when You appear
And every eye shall see You.
Then we shall rise with hearts ablaze
With a song we will sing forever!*

PRAYERS FROM HYMNS

LEAD ME TO CALVARY

JENNIE E. HUSSEY, 1921

King of my life, I crown Thee now,
Thine shall the glory be;
Lest I forget Thy thorn-crowned brow,
Lead me to Calvary.

(Refrain)
Lest I forget Gethsemane;
Lest I forget Thine agony;
Lest I forget Thy love for me,
Lead me to Calvary.

Show me the tomb where Thou wast laid,
Tenderly mourned and wept;
Angels in robes of light arrayed
Guarded Thee whilst Thou slept.

Let me, like Mary thro' the gloom,
Come with a gift to Thee;
Show to me now the empty tomb,
Lead me to Calvary.

May I be willing, Lord, to bear
Daily my cross for Thee;
Even Thy cup of grief to share,
Thou hast borne all for me.

LORD OF LIFE AND KING OF GLORY

CHRISTIAN BURKE, 1904

Lord of life and King of glory,
Who didst deign a child to be,
Cradled on a mother's bosom,
Throned upon a mother's knee:
For the children Thou hast given
We must answer unto Thee.

Grant us then pure hearts and patient,
That in all we do or say
Little ones our deeds may copy,
And be never led astray;
Little feet our steps may follow
In a safe and narrow way.

When our growing sons and daughters
Look on life with eager eyes,
Grant us then a deeper insight
And new pow'rs of sacrifice:
Hope to trust them, faith to guide them,
Love that nothing good denies.

PRAYERS FROM HYMNS

May we keep our holy calling
Stainless in its fair renown,
That, when all the work is over
And we lay the burden down,
Then the children Thou hast given
Still may be our joy and crown.

———— ✤ ✤ ————

[Jesus said,] "Anything is
possible if a person believes."
The father instantly cried
out, "I do believe, but help
me overcome my unbelief!"

MARK 9:23-24

LORD, SPEAK TO ME, THAT I MAY SPEAK

FRANCES R. HAVERGAL, 1872

Lord, speak to me, that I may speak
In living echoes of Thy tone;
As Thou hast sought, so let me seek
Thy erring children lost and lone.

O teach me, Lord, that I may teach
The precious things Thou dost impart;
And wing my words, that they may reach
The hidden depths of many a heart.

O fill me with Thy fullness, Lord,
Until my very heart o'erflow
In kindling thought and glowing word
Thy love to tell, Thy praise to show.

O use me, Lord, use even me,
Just as Thou wilt and when and where;
Until Thy blessed face I see,
Thy rest, Thy joy, Thy glory share.

LOVE DIVINE,
ALL LOVES EXCELLING

CHARLES WESLEY, 1747

Love Divine, all loves excelling,
Joy of heav'n, to earth come down;
Fix in us Thy humble dwelling,
All Thy faithful mercies crown.
Jesus, Thou art all compassion,
Pure, unbounded love Thou art;
Visit us with Thy salvation;
Enter every trembling heart.

Breathe, O breathe Thy loving Spirit
Into every troubled breast!
Let us all in Thee inherit,
Let us find the promised rest.
Take away the love of sinning,
Alpha and Omega be;
End of faith, as its beginning,
Set our hearts at liberty.

Come, Almighty to deliver,
Let us all Thy life receive;
Suddenly return, and never,
Nevermore Thy temples leave:

Thee we would be always blessing,
Serve Thee as Thy hosts above,
Pray, and praise Thee without ceasing,
Glory in Thy perfect love.

Finish then Thy new creation,
Pure and spotless let us be;
Let us see Thy great salvation
Perfectly restored in Thee:
Changed from glory into glory,
Till in heav'n we take our place,
Till we cast our crowns before Thee,
Lost in wonder, love, and praise.

MAY THE MIND
OF CHRIST MY SAVIOR

KATE B. WILKINSON, 1925

May the mind of Christ my Savior
Live in me from day to day,
By His love and pow'r controlling
All I do and say.

May the Word of God dwell richly
In my heart from hour to hour,
So that all may see I triumph
Only through His pow'r.

May the peace of God my Father
Rule my life in everything,
That I may be calm to comfort
Sick and sorrowing.

May the love of Jesus fill me
As the waters fill the sea;
Him exalting, self abasing,
This is victory.

May His beauty rest upon me
As I seek the lost to win,
And may they forget the channel,
Seeing only Him.

To walk with God
we must make
it a practice to talk
with God.

JONI EARECKSON TADA

NOT WHAT THESE HANDS HAVE DONE

HORATIUS BONAR, 1861

Not what these hands have done
Can save this guilty soul;
Not what this toiling flesh has borne
Can make my spirit whole.

Not what I feel or do
Can give me peace with God;
Not all my prayers and sighs and tears
Can bear my awful load.

Thy work alone, O Christ,
Can ease this weight of sin;
Thy blood alone, O Lamb of God,
Can give me peace within.

Thy grace alone, O God,
To me can pardon speak;
Thy power alone, O Son of God,
Can this sore bondage break.

I bless the Christ of God;
I rest on love divine;
And, with unfalt'ring lip and heart,
I call this Savior mine.

O GOD, OUR HELP
IN AGES PAST

ISAAC WATTS, 1719

O God, our help in ages past,
Our hope for years to come,
Our shelter from the stormy blast,
And our eternal home!

Under the shadow of Thy throne
Still may we dwell secure;
Sufficient is Thine arm alone,
And our defense is sure.

Before the hills in order stood,
Or earth received her frame,
From everlasting Thou art God,
To endless years the same.

A thousand ages in Thy sight
Are like an evening gone;
Short as the watch that ends the night,
Before the rising sun.

O God, our help in ages past,
Our hope for years to come,
Be Thou our guide while life shall last,
And our eternal home!

O SACRED HEAD,
NOW WOUNDED

ATTRIBUTED TO BERNARD OF CLAIRVAUX, TWELFTH CENTURY
English Translation by James W. Alexander, 1830

O sacred Head, now wounded,
With grief and shame weighed down,
Now scornfully surrounded
With thorns, Thine only crown:
O sacred Head, what glory,
What bliss till now was Thine!
Yet, though despised and gory,
I joy to call Thee mine.

What Thou, my Lord, hast suffered
Was all for sinners' gain;
Mine, mine was the transgression,
But Thine the deadly pain.
Lo, here I fall, my Savior!
'Tis I deserve Thy place;
Look on me with Thy favor,
Vouchsafe to me Thy grace.

What language shall I borrow
To thank Thee, dearest friend,
For this Thy dying sorrow,
Thy pity without end?
O make me Thine forever;
And should I fainting be,
Lord, let me never, never
Outlive my love to Thee.

———— ✤✤ ————

SAVIOR, LIKE A SHEPHERD LEAD US

ATTRIBUTED TO DOROTHY A. THRUPP, 1836

Savior, like a shepherd lead us,
Much we need Thy tender care;
In Thy pleasant pastures feed us,
For our use Thy folds prepare:
Blessed Jesus, blessed Jesus,
Thou hast bought us, Thine we are;
Blessed Jesus, blessed Jesus,
Thou hast bought us, Thine we are.

We are Thine, do Thou befriend us,
Be the guardian of our way;
Keep Thy flock, from sin defend us,
Seek us when we go astray:
Blessed Jesus, blessed Jesus,
Hear, O hear us when we pray;
Blessed Jesus, blessed Jesus,
Hear, O hear us when we pray.

Thou hast promised to receive us,
Poor and sinful though we be;
Thou hast mercy to relieve us,
Grace to cleanse, and pow'r to free:

Blessed Jesus, blessed Jesus,
Early let us turn to Thee;
Blessed Jesus, blessed Jesus,
Early let us turn to Thee.

Early let us seek Thy favor,
Early let us do Thy will;
Blessed Lord and only Savior,
With Thy love our bosoms fill:
Blessed Jesus, blessed Jesus,
Thou hast loved us, love us still;
Blessed Jesus, blessed Jesus,
Thou hast loved us, love us still.

———— ✦ ✦ ————

SEARCH ME, O GOD

J. EDWIN ORR, 1936

Search me, O God, and know my heart today;
Try me, O Savior, know my thoughts, I pray.
See if there be some wicked way in me;
Cleanse me from every sin and set me free.

I praise Thee, Lord, for cleansing me from sin;
Fulfill Thy Word and make me pure within.
Fill me with fire where once I burned with shame;
Grant my desire to magnify Thy name.

Lord, take my life and make it wholly Thine;
Fill my poor heart with Thy great love divine.
Take all my will, my passion, self, and pride;
I now surrender, Lord—in me abide.

O Holy Spirit, revival comes from Thee;
Send a revival—start the work in me.
Thy Word declares Thou wilt supply our need;
For blessings now, O Lord, I humbly plead.

SPIRIT OF GOD,
DESCEND UPON MY HEART

GEORGE CROLY, 1854

Spirit of God, descend upon my heart;
Wean it from earth, through all its pulses move;
Stoop to my weakness, mighty as Thou art,
And make me love Thee as I ought to love.

I ask no dream, no prophet ecstasies,
No sudden rending of the veil of clay,
No angel visitant, no op'ning skies;
But take the dimness of my soul away.

Hast Thou not bid us love Thee, God and King?
All, all Thine own, soul, heart and strength and mind.
I see Thy cross—there teach my heart to cling:
O let me seek Thee, and O let me find.

Teach me to feel that Thou art always nigh;
Teach me the struggles of the soul to bear,
To check the rising doubt, the rebel sigh;
Teach me the patience of unanswered prayer.

Teach me to love Thee as Thine angels love,
One holy passion filling all my frame;
The baptism of the heav'n-descended Dove,
My heart an altar, and Thy love the flame.

TAKE MY LIFE AND LET IT BE

FRANCES R. HAVERGAL, 1874

Take my life and let it be
Consecrated, Lord, to Thee;
Take my hands and let them move
At the impulse of Thy love,
At the impulse of Thy love.

Take my feet and let them be
Swift and beautiful for Thee;
Take my voice and let me sing
Always, only, for my King,
Always, only, for my King.

Take my lips and let them be
Filled with messages for Thee;
Take my silver and my gold,
Not a mite would I withhold,
Not a mite would I withhold.

Take my love, my God, I pour
At Thy feet its treasure store;
Take myself and I will be
Ever, only, all for Thee,
Ever, only, all for Thee.

WHITER THAN SNOW

JAMES L. NICHOLSON, 1872

Lord Jesus, I long to be perfectly whole;
I want You forever to live in my soul,
Break down every idol, cast out every foe;
Now wash me and I shall be whiter than snow.

(Refrain)
Whiter than snow, yes, whiter than snow;
Now wash me, and I shall be whiter than snow.

Lord Jesus, look down from Your throne in the skies,
And help me to make a complete sacrifice;
I give up myself, and whatever I know,
Now wash me and I shall be whiter than snow.

Lord Jesus for this I most humbly entreat,
I wait, blessed Lord, at Your crucified feet;
By faith, for my cleansing I see Your blood flow,
Now wash me and I shall be whiter than snow.

Lord Jesus, You see that I patiently wait,
Come now, and within me a new heart create;
To those who have sought You, You never said "No,"
Now wash me, and I shall be whiter than snow.

Prayer does not
change God,
but it changes him
who prays.

SØREN KIERKEGAARD

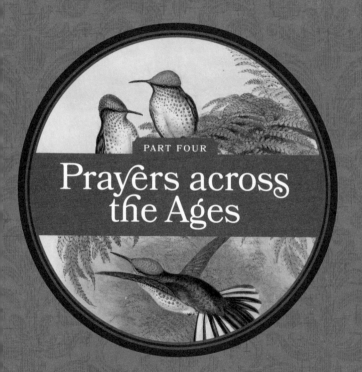

PART FOUR

Prayers across the Ages

BE PRESENT AT OUR TABLE, LORD!

Be present at our table, Lord!
Be here and everywhere adored.
These mercies bless, and grant that we
May strengthened for Thy service be.
 Amen.

BLESS THIS CHILD

A GAELIC CHRISTENING BLESSING

Dearest Father in Heaven,
Bless this child and bless this day of new beginnings.
 Smile upon this child and surround this child,
  Lord, with the soft mantle of Your love.
Teach this child to follow in Your footsteps,
 And to live life in the ways of love, faith, hope,
  and charity.
   Amen.

A CHRISTMAS PRAYER

ROBERT LOUIS STEVENSON (1850–1894)

Loving God,
Help us remember the birth of Jesus,
That we may share in the song of the angels,
The gladness of the shepherds,
And the worship of the wise men.

Close the door of hate
And open the door of love all over the world.
Let kindness come with every gift and good desires
        with every greeting.
Deliver us from evil by the blessing which Christ
        brings,
And teach us to be merry with clear hearts.

May the Christmas morning make us happy to be
        Thy children,
And Christmas evening bring us to our beds with
        grateful thoughts,
Forgiving and forgiven, for Jesus' sake.
    Amen.

DAY BY DAY

Thanks be to Thee, my Lord Jesus Christ,
    For all the benefits Thou hast given me,
    For all the pains and insults Thou has borne
      for me.
O most merciful Redeemer, friend and brother,
    May I know Thee more clearly,
    Love Thee more dearly,
    And follow Thee more nearly,
        Day by day.
        Amen.

May the God of peace make
you holy in every way, and
may your whole spirit
and soul and body be kept
blameless until our Lord
Jesus Christ comes again.

1 THESSALONIANS 5:23

EVENING PRAYER

SAINT MACARIUS (FOURTH CENTURY)

O Eternal God and King of all creation, who hast granted me to arrive at this hour, forgive me the sins that I have committed today in thought, word, and deed, and cleanse, O Lord, my humble soul from all defilement of flesh and spirit. And grant me, O Lord, to pass the sleep of this night in peace, that when I rise from my bed I may please Thy most holy name all the days of my life and conquer my flesh and the fleshless foes that war with me. And deliver me, O Lord, from vain and frivolous thoughts, and from evil desires which defile me. For Thine is the kingdom, the power, and the glory of the Father, Son and Holy Spirit, now and ever, and to the ages of ages. Amen.

FASHIONED FOR JOY

As the hand is made for holding
And the eye for seeing,
You have fashioned me, O Lord, for joy.
Share with me the vision to find that joy everywhere:
In the wild violet's beauty, in the lark's melody,
In the face of a steadfast man, in a child's smile,
In a mother's love, in the purity of Jesus.
    Amen.

FOR PERFECT LOVE

AUGUSTINE (354–430)

Look upon us, O Lord,
And let all the darkness of our souls
   Vanish before the beams of Thy brightness.
Fill us with holy love,
   And open to us the treasures of Thy wisdom.
All our desire is known unto Thee;
    Therefore perfect what Thou hast begun,
    And what Thy Spirit has awakened us to ask
      in prayer.
We seek Thy face;
   Turn Thy face unto us and show us Thy glory.
Then shall our longing be satisfied,
   And our peace shall be perfect.
      Amen.

GOD IS GREAT, GOD IS GOOD

A CHILD'S MEALTIME BLESSING

God is great, God is good.
Let us thank Him for our food.
By His hands we all are fed.
Give us, Lord, our daily bread.
　　Amen.

———— ✣ ✤ ————

GOD OF LOVE, GIVE US LOVE

WILLIAM TEMPLE (1881–1944)

O God of love, we ask You to give us love:
Love in our thinking, love in our speaking, love in
our doing,
And love in the hidden places of our souls;
Love of our neighbours near and far;
Love of our friends old and new;
Love of those with whom we might find it hard
to bear,
And love of those who find it hard to bear with us;
Love of those with whom we work,
And love of those with whom we take our ease;
Love in joy, love in sorrow;
Love in life and love in death;
That so at length we may dwell with You,
Who are eternal love.
Amen.

GOOD-NIGHT PRAYER FOR A LITTLE CHILD

HENRY JOHNSTONE (1835–1907)

Father, unto Thee I pray,
Thou hast guarded me all day;
Safe I am while in Thy sight,
Safely let me sleep tonight.

Bless my friends, the whole world bless;
Help me to learn helpfulness;
Keep me ever in Thy sight;
So to all I say good night.
    Amen.

GRANT ME PEACE OF SOUL

PETER AINSLIE (1867–1934)

Father, You have shown me wonderful things out of Your Word. You have set me in a new position—my relationship to You is closer and more blessed than I knew. Your Holy Spirit has made me Your child, and taken my otherwise fruitless life and made it the ground tilled by your hand.

Grant to me such peace of soul that I may be calm amid all vexation, that I may find my highest joy in abiding in Christ, that I may be called by You Your friend and may live in a conscious oneness both with You and all who love You in sincerity. Have mercy upon Your divided Church and heal the breach for Jesus' sake, that the world may believe that You did send him. Amen.

HEAR MY PRAYER, O HEAVENLY FATHER

HARRIET PARR (1828–1900)

Hear my prayer, O heavenly Father,
    Ere I lay me down to sleep;
Bid Thy angels, pure and holy,
    Round my bed their vigil keep.

My sins are heavy, but Thy mercy
    Far outweighs them, every one;
Down before Thy cross I cast them,
    Trusting in Thy help alone.

None shall measure out Thy patience
    By the span of human thought;
None shall bound the tender mercies
    Which Thy holy Son has bought.

Pardon all my past transgressions,
    Give me strength for days to come;
Guide and guard me with Thy blessing
    Till Thy angels bid me home.*
        Amen.

---

* This poem by Victorian novelist Harriet Parr was included in a Christmas story by
Charles Dickens, published in his periodical *Household Words*. The poem was
subsequently put to music as a hymn that first appeared in the *New Congregational
Hymn Book* in 1859.

God will not compete
for our attention. We
must arrange time for our
communion with Him.

DALLAS WILLARD

ᴀ HEART FOR THEE

O Lord, who hast mercy upon all,
Take away from me my sins,
    And mercifully kindle in me the fire of
        Thy Holy Spirit.
Take away from me the heart of stone,
    And give me a heart of flesh,
           A heart to love and adore Thee,
           A heart to delight in Thee,
    To follow and to enjoy Thee,
For Christ's sake, amen.

IN NEED OF FILLING

MARTIN LUTHER (1483–1546)

Behold, Lord, an empty vessel that needs to be filled. My Lord, fill it. I am weak in faith; strengthen Thou me. I am cold in love; warm me and make me fervent that my love may go out to my neighbor. I do not have a strong and firm faith; at times I doubt and am unable to trust Thee altogether. O Lord, help me. Strengthen my faith and trust in Thee. In Thee I have sealed the treasures of all I have. I am poor; Thou art rich and didst come to be merciful to the poor. I am a sinner; Thou art upright. With me there is an abundance of sin; in Thee is the fullness of righteousness. Therefore, I will remain with Thee, of who I can receive, but to whom I may not give. Amen.

JESUS, FRIEND OF LITTLE CHILDREN

WALTER JOHN MATHAMS (1853–1931)

Jesus, Friend of little children,
Be a friend to me;
Take my hand, and ever keep me
Close to Thee.

Teach me how to grow in goodness,
Daily as I grow;
Thou hast been a child, and surely
Thou dost know.

Step by step O lead me onward,
Upward into youth;
Wiser, stronger, still becoming
In Thy truth.

Never leave me, nor forsake me;
Ever be my friend;
For I need Thee, from life's dawning
To its end.
Amen.

A KING LIKE NO OTHER

ATTRIBUTED TO EPHRAEM OF SYRIA (CA. 306–373)

Child of Bethlehem, what contrasts You embrace! No one has ever been so humble; no one has ever wielded such power. We stand in awe of Your holiness, and yet we are bathed in Your love.

And where shall we look for You? You are in high heaven, in the glory of the Godhead. Yet those who searched for You on earth found You in a tiny baby at Mary's breast. We come in hushed reverence to find You as God, and You welcome us as man. We come unthinkingly to find You as man, and are blinded by the light of Your Godhead.

You are the heir to King David's throne, but You renounced all his royal splendor. Of all his luxurious bedrooms, You chose a stable. Of all his magnificent beds, You chose a feeding trough. Of all his golden chariots, You chose an ass.

Never was there a king like you! Instead of royal isolation, You made Yourself available to everyone who needed You. Instead of high security, You made Yourself vulnerable to those who hated You.

It is we who need You, above anything in the world. You give Yourself to us with such total generosity, that it might almost seem that You need us. There never was a king like this before! Amen.

LORD, BE WITH US

SAINT PATRICK (CA. 386–461)

Lord, be with us this day,
Within us to purify us;
Above us to draw us up;
Beneath us to sustain us;
Before us to lead us;
Behind us to restrain us;
Around us to protect us.
    Amen.

LOVE OF MY HEART

AMY CARMICHAEL (1867–1951)

Love of my heart, my stream runs dry,
O Fountain of the heavenly hills,
Love, blessed Love, to Thee I cry,
Flood all my secret hidden rills,
Waters of love, oh pour through me;
I must have love—I must have Thee!*
Amen.

——— ❧❧ ———

MORNING PRAYER: A GENERAL CONFESSION

THE BOOK OF COMMON PRAYER, 1928

Almighty and most merciful Father,
> We have erred, and strayed from Thy ways like lost sheep.
> We have followed too much the devices and desires of our own hearts.
> We have offended against Thy holy laws.
> We have left undone those things which we ought to have done;
> And we have done those things which we ought not to have done;
>> And there is no health in us.
> But Thou, O Lord, have mercy upon us, miserable offenders.
> Spare Thou those, O God, who confess their faults.
> Restore Thou those who are penitent;
>> According to Thy promises declared unto mankind in Christ Jesus our Lord.
> And grant, O most merciful Father, for His sake;
> That we may hereafter live a godly, righteous, and sober life,
> To the glory of Thy holy Name. Amen.

PEACE PRAYER

ATTRIBUTED TO SAINT FRANCIS OF ASSISI (1181–1226)

Lord, make me an instrument of Your peace;
    Where there is hatred, let me sow love;
    Where there is injury, pardon;
    Where there is doubt, faith;
    Where there is despair, hope;
    Where there is darkness, light;
    Where there is sadness, joy.
O Divine Master, grant that I may not so much seek
    To be consoled as to console;
    To be understood as to understand;
    To be loved as to love.
For it is in giving that we receive;
    It is in pardoning that we are pardoned;
    It is in dying that we are born to eternal life.
        Amen.

PRAISE TO OUR WONDER-WORKING GOD

ATTRIBUTED TO SAINT FRANCIS OF ASSISI (1181–1226)

You are holy, Lord God, who alone works wonders. You are strong. You are great. You are most high. You are the almighty King, You, holy Father, King of heaven and earth. You are the Lord God Triune and One; all good. You are good, all good, the highest good, Lord God living and true. You are love, charity. You are wisdom. You are humility. You are patience. You are security. You are quietude. You are joy and gladness. You are justice and temperance. You are all riches to sufficiency. You are beauty. You are meekness. You are our protector. You are our guardian and defender. You are strength. You are refreshment. You are our hope. You are our faith. You are our great sweetness. You are our eternal life great and admirable Lord, God Almighty, merciful Savior. Amen.

PRAYER BEFORE READING SCRIPTURE

AUGUSTUS TOPLADY (1740–1778)

Teach us, O Lord, the way of Your statutes, and make us keep it unto the end. Incline our hearts to Your testimonies, and cause us to go in the path of Your commandments, for therein is our desire. May the law of Your mouth be dearer unto us than thousands of gold and silver; and let Your Holy Spirit accompany Your Word with saving power to our souls, through Jesus Christ our Lord. Amen.

A PRAYER FOR DISCERNMENT

THOMAS À KEMPIS (1380–1471)

Grant me, O Lord, the grace to know what should be known, to praise what is most pleasing to You, to esteem that which appears most precious to You, and to abhor what is unclean in Your sight.

Do not allow me to judge according to the light of my bodily eyes, nor to give sentence according to the hearing of ignorant men's ears. But let me distinguish with true judgment between things visible and spiritual, and always seek above all things Your good pleasure. Amen.

PRAYER FOR PEACE AMONG NATIONS

WILLIAM TEMPLE (1881–1944)

O Almighty God, the Father of all humanity,
Turn, we pray, the hearts of all peoples and their
     rulers,
That by the power of Your Holy Spirit
Peace may be established among the nations
On the foundation of justice, righteousness, and
     truth;
Through Him who was lifted up on the cross
To draw all people to Himself,
Your Son, Jesus Christ our Lord. Amen.

A PRAYER OF THANKS

EDITH RUTTER LEATHAM (TWENTIETH CENTURY)

Thank You for the world so sweet,
Thank You for the food we eat,
Thank You for the birds that sing,
Thank You, God, for everything.
    Amen.

SAFE WITHIN THY HAND

COLUMBA (521–597)

Alone with none but Thee, my God,
    I journey on my way.
What need I fear when Thou art near
    O King of night and day?
More safe am I within Thy hand
    Than if a host did round me stand.
        Amen.

SERENITY PRAYER

REINHOLD NIEBUHR (1892–1971)

God, grant me the serenity to accept the things
    I cannot change,
Courage to change the things I can,
And wisdom to know the difference.
    Amen.

THANKS FOR FOOD
IN A WORLD OF HUNGER

AUTHOR UNKNOWN

For food in a world where many walk in hunger;
For faith in a world where many walk in fear;
For friends in a world where many walk alone;
We give You thanks, O Lord.
    Amen.

THANKSGIVING PRAYER

RALPH WALDO EMERSON (1803–1882)

For each new morning with its light,
    For rest and shelter of the night,
For health and food, for love and friends,
    For everything Thy goodness sends.
        Amen.

TO GOD WHO GIVES OUR DAILY BREAD

THOMAS TALLIS (CA. 1505–1585)

To God who gives our daily bread
    A thankful song we raise,
And pray that He who sends us food
    May fill our hearts with praise.
        Amen.

UNTIL WE MEET AGAIN

May the road rise up to meet you.
May the wind be always at your back.
May the sun shine warm upon your face,
And rains fall soft upon your fields.
And until we meet again,
May God hold you in the palm of His hand.
    Amen.

WASH MY FEET

ORIGEN (185–254)

Jesus, my feet are dirty. Come even as a slave to me, pour water into your bowl, come and wash my feet. In asking such a thing I know I am overbold, but I dread what was threatened when You said to me, "If I do not wash your feet I have no fellowship with you." Wash my feet then, because I long for Your companionship. Amen.

WEDDING PRAYER

WENDELL C. HAWLEY

Lord of love,
Bless this man and this woman as, mysteriously and
      wonderfully, they now are pledged as one.
By the power of your Holy Spirit pour out the
      abundance of Your blessing upon this new
      home, now established in Christ Jesus.
Give them health, strength, and wisdom to provide
      for the necessities of life, but let them be not
      so consumed with the getting that they are
      overtaken by the cares of life.
Give them a great capacity for tenderness,
    an unusual gift of understanding,
      a willingness to overlook each other's weaknesses
      and see each other's strengths.
Give them an ever-growing love and fidelity that
      overcomes the hazardous terrain of life's
      journey.
Give them a faith in your purposes—so strong that
      they will trust You no matter what the future
      holds.

May _____ and _____ experience the
    promise of God to Abraham,
I will bless you . . . and you shall be a blessing.
May all who enter their home leave spiritually
    enriched and blessed.
Thank you, heavenly Father, for Your presence here
    with us and for Your promised blessing upon
    us, all the days of our lives.
        Amen.[*]

[*] Wendell Hawley, *A Pastor Prays for His People* (Carol Stream, IL: Tyndale House
  Publishers, 2010), 162.

YOUR ARM OF STRENGTH AND HEART OF PITY

PETER AINSLIE (1867–1934)

O Shepherd, You have revealed to me Your arm of strength and Your heart of pity. Your voice is to me sweeter than music, and Your presence inflames my soul. I know that You are the truth, and that out of my grave I shall leap to meet You with joy. You are my Guardian as I walk this human pathway, and You are my Hope as I look above. Out of Your sacrifice has come my redemption, and out of Your obedience has come my pardon. The bread of life is my food and the water of life is my drink, and beneath the light of Your love I adore and magnify Your holy name. Amen.

Storm the throne
of grace, and persevere
therein, and mercy
will come down.

JOHN WESLEY

Topical Index

———— ✦✦ ————

The LORD is close to all
who call on him,
yes, to all who call
on him in truth.

PSALM 145:18